Issues in Employee Leave

Allan H. Weitzman
Xan Raskin

Proskauer Rose LLP
One Boca Place, Suite 340
2255 Glades Road
Boca Raton, FL 33431-7383

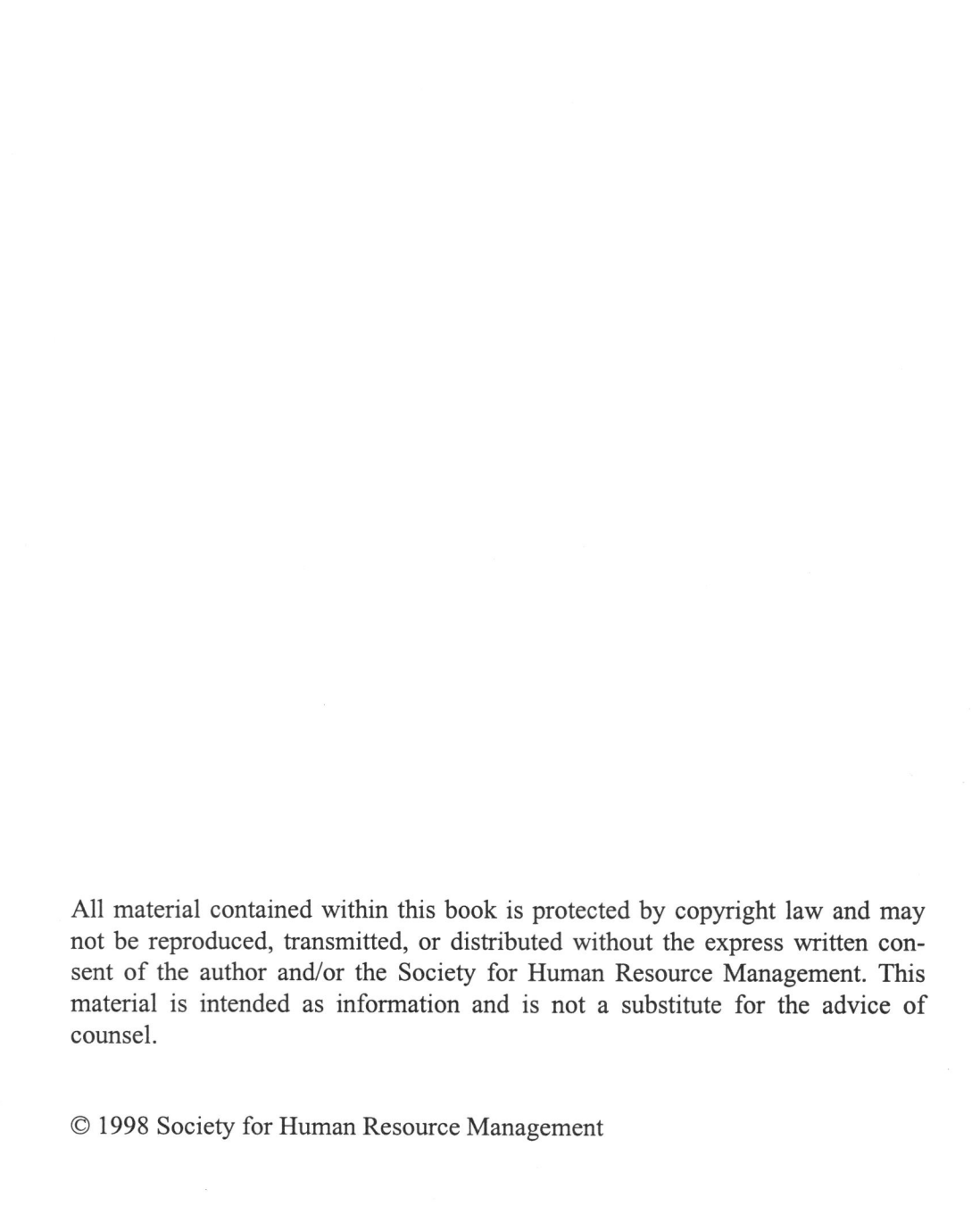

All material contained within this book is protected by copyright law and may not be reproduced, transmitted, or distributed without the express written consent of the author and/or the Society for Human Resource Management. This material is intended as information and is not a substitute for the advice of counsel.

© 1998 Society for Human Resource Management

This book is published by the Society for Human Resource Management (SHRM) and funded by a grant from the SHRM Foundation. The interpretations, conclusions and recommendations, however, are those of the author, and do not necessarily represent those of the Foundation or of SHRM.

About the Authors: *Allan H. Weitzman* is a Partner at Proskauer Rose LLP, and is head of the Labor and Employment Law Department in its Boca Raton office. He is a member of the Bar in New York and Florida, and frequently represents employers in state and federal court on employment and labor issues. He often speaks on these issues at SHRM meetings and conferences, has authored countless articles, and is the Edior-in-Chief of a bimonthly journal, *HR Advisor—Legal and Practical Guidance,* published by Warren, Gorham & Lamont. *Xan Raskin* is an Associate at Proskauer Rose in the Labor and Employment Law Department at New York office.

The Society for Human Resource Management (SHRM) is the leading voice of the human resource profession. SHRM, which celebrates its 50th anniversary in 1998, provides education and information services, conferences and seminars, government and media representation, online services and publications to more than 100,000 professional and student members throughout the world. The Society, the world's largest human resource management association, is a founding member of the North American Human Resource Management Association (NAHRMA) and a founding member and Secretariat of the World Federation of Personnel Management Associations (WFPMA). On behalf of NAHRMA, SHRM also serves as President of WFPMA.

ISBN 0-939900-88-2

TABLE OF CONTENTS

Table of Contents iv

Chapter 1 Introduction 1
    Why It's Practical to Have a Leave Policy 1
    Types of Leave an Employer Can Establish... 1
    Factors to Consider When Developing and Issuing a Leave Policy 2

PART ONE: STATUTORY LEAVES

Chapter 2 Federal Family and Medical Leave.. 3
    Introduction 3
    Covered Employers and Employee Eligibility 3
    Events That May Entitle an Employee to FMLA Leave 4
    How Much FMLA Leave May Be Taken? 5
    Substitution of Paid Leave 6
    Intermittent Leave 6
    Husband and Wife Employed by Employer 7
    How Is FMLA Leave Requested and Scheduled? 7
    Interim Health Benefits 9
    Employee Reinstatement after Leave 10
    Notice Requirements for Employers 11

Chapter 3 State and Local Family and Medical Leaves of Absence 13
    State Laws 13
        New Jersey 13
        Connecticut.. 14
        District of Columbia 14
        California... 15
        Florida 15
    County and Local Laws.. 15

Chapter 4   Pregnancy Disability and Child Care Leave 17
Mandatory Federal Leave 17
State Laws 18
    California 18
    Florida 19
    New York 19
    Maryland 19
    District of Columbia 19

Chapter 5   Leave under the Americans with Disabilities Act 21
Introduction 21
Employer Coverage 21
Individual Coverage 22
Discrimination 22
Disabilities Covered by the ADA 22
Essential Functions 23
The "Reasonable Accommodation" Obligation 24
Leave as a Reasonable Accommodation 25
The Length of the ADA Leave 25
Excessive Absenteeism 26
Leaves Relating to Substance or Alcohol Abuse 27

Chapter 6   Workers' Compensation Leaves 29
Coping with Return-to-Work Issues 29

Chapter 7   The Interplay among the ADA, FMLA, and
                Workers' Compensation: Answers to Practical,
                Difficult Leave Issues 31
ADA and FMLA 31
    Eligibility and Amount of Leave 31
    Permissible Medical Information and Documentation Requests 32
    Employee Transfers 34
    Reinstatement Issues 34
    Intermittent Leave or Reduced Schedule Issues 35
    No-Fault Policies 35
FMLA and Workers' Compensation 36
    Employer Management Issues 36
ADA and Workers' Compensation 37
    Defining Disability 37
    Disability-Related Questions and Examinations 37
    Reasonable Accommodations 38
    Returning to Work 39
    Reassignment and Transfer 40
    Light Duty Positions 40

  Preexisting Conditions 40
  Disability Benefits 41

Chapter 8 Military Leaves of Absence 43
 USERRA 43
  Covered Employers 43
  Covered Employees 44
  Covered Military Services 44
 Benefit Entitlement and Reemployment Rights 44
 Reapplication Requirements for Employment upon Return 46
 Military Leave Policies 47
 VEVRA 47
 State Laws 47
  Florida 48
  New York 48
  California 48

Chapter 9 Jury, Witness, and Voting Duty 49
 Jury Duty 49
  Employer Requirements 49
  Employee Obligations 49
  Postponement of Jury Duty 50
  Payment of Salary during Duty 50
  Work Schedule during Duty 50
 Witness Duty 50
 Voting Duty 51

Chapter 10 Religious Leave 53
 Reasonable Accommodations under Title VII 53

PART TWO: LEAVE AS AN EMPLOYEE BENEFIT

Chapter 11 Disability Leave 57
 Short-Term Disability Leave 57
 Long-Term Disability Leave 57
 Salary Continuation Policies 58

Chapter 12 Employee Assistance Programs 59

Chapter 13 Paid Leaves 61
 Vacation Leave 61
 Sick Leave 62

Comprehensive Leave 63
Personal Leave or Bereavement Leave 63
Time Banks 63
Holiday Leave 64
Sabbaticals.. 64
Union-Related Leave Issues 65
    Employer Obligations Regarding Leave to Conduct Union Business...................... 65
    Prohibitions on Pay and Benefits during Union Leave 65
    Potential Liability for Providing Pay and Benefits during Union Leave................. 65
    The Establishment of Leave Benefits under Collective Bargaining Agreements..... 66
    The Overlay of the ADA and FMLA on the Collective Bargaining Process 66
Meals and Rest Periods 67

PART THREE: IMPLEMENTING LEAVE PROCEDURES

Chapter 14   Implementation Procedures 69
Expressing Leave Policy Components 69
    Employee Handbooks 69
    Other Communication Tools 70
Dissemination of Leave Policies 70

Chapter 15   Addressing Implementation Policy Options... 71
Developing Procedures that an Employee Must Follow When Requesting Leave 71
Oral and Written Requests for Leave 71
Medical Benefit Continuation during Leave 71
Seniority Accrual during Leave 72
Vacation and Benefit Credits.. 72
Addressing Leave Policy Abuse... 72
Reemployment Entitlements 73
Leave Cancellation... 73
The Effect of Layoffs on Leave 73
Setting Time Limits on Leave 74

Appendix A   Sample Policy Statements and Handbook Provisions 75

Appendix B   Sample Employer Response to Employee Request for
                    Familyor Medical Leave 87

Appendix C   Certification of Health Care Provider 93

Appendix D Types of Leave 101
　Short-Term Disability Benefits 101
　Military Leave 102
　Jury & Witness Duty 103
　Voting Leave 104
　Vacation Leave 105
　Guidelines for Vacation Pay upon Termination 106
　Absence Due to Illness 107
　Bereavement Leave 108
　Personal Leave (Paid) 109
　Personal Leave (Unpaid) 109
　Holidays 111

CHAPTER 1

INTRODUCTION

Why It's Practical to Have a Leave Policy

As quality of life issues percolate within the workplace, employee leave policies have assumed a greater importance. In fact, employees and applicants often judge employers by their leave policies. It's no secret that the most frequently read section of an employee handbook is the one describing vacations!

But it's not just a one-way street. Employers also benefit from the establishment of leave policies. The nature and breadth of policies can set the tone for a company's values and culture and can stimulate employee morale and loyalty. For example, not only are employees less productive if they are forced to work during a crucial personal emergency; but also granting leave for emergencies makes employees aware that their employers care about their overall well-being. The trick, however, is to find a balance of policies that are not too restrictive and yet protect against leave abuse.

Types of Leave an Employer Can Establish

When the time comes to formulate a leave policy, employers are not working on a blank slate. While most employers grant employees different kinds of leaves of absence, many are mandated by federal, state, and local laws. Such benefits are covered in "Part One: Statutory Leaves," which discusses leaves for family and medical, pregnancy, disability, workers' compensation, military, jury duty, witness duty, voting duty, and religious accommodation.

"Part Two: Leave as an Employee Benefit" describes the various leave benefits that are on the optional menu for employers, including long- and short-term disability, vacations, personal leave, bereavement leave, holidays, sabbaticals, union-related leave, and meals and rest periods.

Although employers can often choose between granting leave as paid or unpaid, providing compensation during several types of both statutory and optional leave is a common practice among most companies. To remain competitive, employers should both examine and compare their leave policies with those of their counterparts. If recruiting and retaining the right people for the business turns on the quality-of-life advantages that are offered, granting paid leave will often benefit the employer enough to offset the cost of lost wages. An additional option is to incorporate flextime, work at home, or job sharing into existing paid or unpaid leave policies.

Factors to Consider When Developing and Issuing a Leave Policy

Because many types of leave are mandated by statute, "Part Three: Implementing Leave Policies" discusses how employers should be aware that the legal requirements at the federal, state, and local levels must be followed in developing such policies. For leaves that are granted as employee benefits, policy statements must be drafted carefully because they may create contractual obligations and because employers should be prepared to be bound by the terms they select. (Some of the common legal considerations in drafting these provisions are discussed later.)

A personnel handbook is the best medium for employers to communicate to their employees both the leave policies that are required by statute and those that are established to benefit employees (such as vacation and employee assistance plans). Handbook leave policies need to be clear, concise, and flexible enough to accommodate the varying needs of employees, as the policy statement's degree of formality will set the tone for the amount of flexibility in the administration of policies.

All employees should receive policy statements and handbooks immediately upon beginning employment, and employers should make sure that all supervisors and managers are familiar with both the terms and the application of the policies. Employers should also provide employees with several opportunities to discuss leave policies so that employees not only receive but also understand the provisions.

PART ONE: STATUTORY LEAVES

Chapter 2

Federal Family and Medical Leave

Introduction

If someone asked for a two-sentence summary of the federal Family and Medical Leave Act (FMLA), it would be the following: FMLA generally requires covered private employers and public agencies to provide eligible employees with up to 12 weeks in a 12-month period away from work for birth, adoption, child care, and serious health conditions of the employees or of family members. During FMLA leave, employers are typically required to maintain the employees' pre-existing group health insurance coverage and to restore the employees to the same or an equivalent position at the end of the FMLA leave.

Unfortunately, the law is not that simple. In addition to the statute itself, the U.S. Department of Labor issued final regulations that went into effect on April 6, 1995. The details of these regulations are too extensive to include in this book. However, on the following pages we have outlined most of the key statutory and regulatory provisions.

Covered Employers and Employee Eligibility

Employers with fewer than 50 employees may skip the rest of this chapter, unless they want to learn what lies ahead as they cross the magic growth line from 49 to 50. Employers who have 50 or more employees are covered by the FMLA and must grant leave to their "eligible employees."

Fortunately, not every employee is eligible for leave under the FMLA. The law requires that employees must have been employed by the employer (a) for at least 12 months, which need not be consecutive; (b) for at least 1,250 hours of service during the 12-month period immediately preceding the beginning of FMLA leave; and (c) at a worksite where there are 50 or more employees within a 75-mile radius.

If the employer does not maintain accounting records of the actual hours that an employee worked (as, for example, in the case of an employee who is exempt under the Fair Labor Standards Act), the employer has the burden of showing that the employee has worked fewer than the requisite 1,250 hours of service. If the employer cannot meet this burden, the U.S. Department of Labor presumes that the employee has met the eligibility requirement.

Events That May Entitle an Employee to FMLA Leave

Employees may take an FMLA leave for the following reasons:

- the birth of a child (including prenatal care) and to care for the newborn child;
- the placement with the employee of a child for adoption or foster care and to care for the child;
- to care for the employee's spouse, child, or parent (but not in-law) with a serious health condition; and/or
- the employee's own serious health condition that renders the employee unable to perform the essential functions of the employee's job.

To date, leave for reasons of birth or adoption has not been the primary source of either legal or practical problems in deciding entitlement. For the human resources practitioner, the greatest difficulty lies in determining whether the employee's ailment is one that meets the definition of a "serious health condition."

A "serious health condition" is defined by the FMLA as an illness, injury, impairment, or physical or mental condition that involves an inpatient stay in a hospital, hospice, or residential medical care facility, or continuing treatment by a health care provider. A "serious health condition" also includes a period of incapacity of more than 3 consecutive calendar days that also involves (a) treatment two or more times; or (b) treatment on at least one occasion that results in a regimen of continuing treatment; any period of incapacity caused by pregnancy or for prenatal care; a chronic condition requiring treatments (for example, asthma, diabetes, or epilepsy); a permanent or long-term condition requiring supervision (for example, Alzheimer's, a severe stroke, or the terminal stages of a disease); or multiple treatments of a nonchronic condition (for example, cancer—chemotherapy, radiation, etc.; severe arthritis—physical therapy; or kidney disease—dialysis).

While the conditions that were just mentioned are all presumed to be "serious health conditions," the list is hardly an exhaustive one. The definition of serious health condition does not generally cover the following minor illnesses: the common cold, the flu, earaches, upset stomach, minor ulcers, headaches (other than migraine), routine dental or orthodontia problems, and periodontal disease. If, however, any of these conditions meet the regulatory criteria for a serious health condition (for example, an incapacity of more than 3 consecutive days and treatment by a health care provider on at least one occasion resulting in a regimen of continuing treatment), the absence would be covered by the FMLA. Mental illness resulting from stress, allergies, or treatment for substance abuse *may* be considered a serious health condition *only* if the condition involves inpatient care or continuing treatment (as defined by the regulations). In addition, a cosmetic treatment is not covered as a "serious health condition" unless inpatient hospital care is required or complications develop.

How Much FMLA Leave May Be Taken?

An eligible employee may take up to 12 workweeks of unpaid leave during the 12-month period for any one, or combination, of the above-described entitling situations. Although the Department of Labor allows for a number of methods to calculate the "12-month period" (including the calendar year, fiscal year, employee's anniversary year, and rolling forward year), many employers feel it is most protective of their rights to choose the 12-month period immediately preceding the commencement of any FMLA leave (commonly known as the "rolling" backward 12-month period). This choice, although somewhat difficult to administer without the proper software, will prevent employees from taking the two back-to-back 12-week leaves that are possible under any other method of calculation. An employer who does not designate the method of calculating the 12-month period will be forced to use the method that is most advantageous to the employee. FMLA leave for childbirth or adoption/foster care placement must conclude 12 months after the birth or placement of the child unless the employer authorizes otherwise.

Substitution of Paid Leave

Whether FMLA is to be paid or unpaid is another issue where the law gives the employer policy-making options. FMLA is generally unpaid leave, but an employer may require, or the employee may elect, to substitute certain accrued paid leave for unpaid FMLA leave. An employer may also require an employee to use all qualifying accrued paid leave for FMLA purposes before making unpaid leave available. If, however, the employee is on disability or workers' compensation and FMLA leave, neither the employee nor the employer is allowed to substitute any accrued paid leave during this time.

If an employee elects to substitute accrued paid leave for the unpaid leave provided under the FMLA, the substituted leave must be both earned and available for use by the employee. The substitution of paid leave for unpaid leave does not entitle the employee to extend the 12-workweek leave period by law. Thus, if an employee requests leave to care for a child with a serious health condition, and requests 2 weeks accrued paid vacation time followed by 12 weeks of unpaid FMLA leave, the employer need only grant a total of 12 workweeks of leave (that is, 2 weeks paid and 10 weeks unpaid FMLA leave).

If the employer requires paid leave to be substituted for unpaid FMLA leave, the employer must convey this decision to the employee within 2 business days after the employee gives notice of the leave or after the employer has determined that the leave qualifies as FMLA leave.

Intermittent Leave

Unfortunately, the greatest potential source of employer frustration and employee abuse is the intermittent leave requirement. Theoretically, an employee with migraine headaches (a "serious health condition") can call in for FMLA every Monday of the year, plus 8 more Fridays. And, in the absence of fraud, there would be little that an employer could do to prevent this leave time.

This problem arises because an employer must allow an employee to take intermittent leave or work on a reduced schedule if there is a medical need for the leave (as distinguished from voluntary treatments and procedures) that can be best accommodated through an intermittent or reduced leave schedule. In these cases, employees must attempt to schedule their leave so as not to disrupt employers' operations. An employer may also assign an employee to an alternative position (with equivalent pay and benefits) that better accommodates the employee's intermittent or reduced leave schedule.

An employer is not required to allow an employee to take leave for birth, placement of a child, or child care, either intermittently or on a reduced work schedule. (Of course, if an employee's pregnancy is a "serious health condition" (including morning sickness), the normal rules about intermittent leave apply.)

Husband and Wife Employed by Employer

If a husband and wife are both employed by the same employer, they can take together only a combined total of 12 weeks of FMLA leave within the "12-month period" for any childbirth or placement or to care for a seriously ill parent. They can split the leave between them in any proportions. Each spouse may be entitled to additional FMLA leave for other qualifying reasons (that is, the difference between the days or weeks of leave taken individually for childbirth, for placement, or to care for a seriously ill parent and 12 weeks, but not more than a total of 12 weeks per person). For example, if each spouse took 6 weeks of FMLA leave to care for a newborn child, each could later use an additional six weeks to care for a sick child or for his/her own serious illness.

How Is FMLA Leave Requested and Scheduled?

If the leave is foreseeable, an employee must provide the employer with at least 30 days' advance notice before the FMLA leave is to begin. If 30 days' notice is not practicable or if the leave is unforeseeable, the employee must give the employer notice as soon as is practicable under the facts and circumstances of the particular case. It is expected that the employee will notify the employer within no more than 1 or 2 working days after learning of the need for leave, unless there are extraordinary circumstances that make this notification infeasible.

Written notification from the employee is not required under the FMLA regulations. Employees are required, however, to provide the employer with at least verbal notification of their need to take leave. In addition, employees are not required to expressly assert their rights under the FMLA, and they do not have to mention the FMLA. Employees must state only that leave is needed for a qualifying reason, and the employer is then expected to obtain any additional information that may be required. It is, however, required that employees provide this additional information when it can readily be accomplished, taking into consideration any exigent circumstances. An employer may also require that the need for the leave be supported by a certification issued by the health care provider of the employee or of the employee's ill family member. (For a fuller discussion of the FMLA's restrictions on an employer's right to challenge the certification, see chapter 7.)

Generally, employers should notify employees that leave has been designated FMLA leave before it starts and should provide employees with certain specific advance notices. (Under certain limited circumstances discussed below, leave may be designated retroactively.) When an employer has knowledge of the reason for leave, but fails to designate, the employer may not designate retroactively and may designate only prospectively from the date that notification was provided to the employee. Even though the employer may not designate retroactively, the employee is subject to the full protections of the FMLA during the entire period. In other words, in the absence of designation, the employee gets all the FMLA benefits but the time away from work does not count against the employee's 12-week maximum.

There are two scenarios under which an employer may designate leave as FMLA after an employee returns to work. First, when the employer learns of the reason for the absence only after the employee's return to work, the employer may, within 2 business days of the employee's return, designate the leave retroactively with appropriate notice to the employee. Second, if the employer knows the reason for the leave, but has not been able to confirm that the leave qualifies as FMLA or has not yet received medical certification or second or third medical opinions, the employer may preliminarily or provisionally designate the leave as FMLA leave. A preliminary designation becomes final once the employer has received the requisite information confirming that the leave is for an FMLA reason. If the medical certification fails to confirm that the absence was for an FMLA reason, the employer must withdraw the provisional designation with written notice to the employee. Employers should get into the habit of preliminarily or provisionally designating leave as FMLA leave. This anticipatory designation enables employers to capture the full amount of FMLA leave and avoids retroactive designation problems.

Employers may give oral or written notice of the FMLA designation to employees, but oral notice must be confirmed in writing no later than the next payday to occur 1 week or more after the oral notice. To prevent employees from taking more than 12 weeks, an employer can, and should, count an employee's absence as FMLA leave if it meets all of the requirements, even if the employee does not desire or request that the absence be designated as FMLA.

Interim Health Benefits

Employers must maintain coverage under their group health plan for the duration of an employee's FMLA leave at the level and under the conditions that this coverage would have been provided if the employee had continued employment. An employer is not required to continue to provide a cash supplement that was provided in lieu of health benefits. Additionally, the employer may not offer the employee options in lieu of maintenance of group health plan coverage during any period of FMLA leave.

For the portion of FMLA leave that is unpaid, the employees are responsible for payment of their portion of health insurance premiums during the leave, as if they were still on the payroll. (An employer can require an employee to pay only for interim health benefits if the employer requires payments from other employees on unpaid leave, and the same payment rules apply to FMLA-interim health insurance as if the employee is on any other leave without pay.) Employers must provide employees who are on FMLA with advance notice of the costs and a schedule to pay the interim health insurance premiums. This payment schedule may include paying a share of the premium payments

- at the same time as would be made by payroll deduction;
- on the same schedule as COBRA payments (COBRA requires employers that maintain group health plans for employees to permit them to elect "continuation coverage" at their own expense, following certain qualifying events that would otherwise cause them to lose group coverage);
- on a prepaid basis pursuant to a cafeteria plan at the employee's option;
- according to the employer's rules for leave without pay as long as no prepayment of premiums is required; or
- according to a system voluntarily agreed to between the employer and the employee, which may include prepayment of premiums.

If an employee's premium payment for interim health insurance is more than 30 days late, the employer's obligation to continue health care coverage ceases after the employer gives 15 days' written notice. If the employee's health coverage is discontinued during the leave because the employee has not made the required interim payment(s) while on FMLA leave, then after the employee's return from FMLA leave, health benefits must be restored to the employee as if the leave had not been taken and the premium payment(s) had not been missed. The employee cannot be required to meet any requalification requirements imposed by the plan. To overcome a requalification requirement, the employer may continue to pay the employee's share of any health premium(s) missed by the employee during the FMLA leave period. Assuming that the employee returns to work, the employer may then recover the employee's share of the missed premium payment(s) through subsequent payroll deductions.

During FMLA leave, no accrual or continuation of any other benefits is required. If, however, other employees on leave without pay accrue additional benefits, or seniority, those benefits must be provided to the employee on unpaid FMLA leave. (The employer may elect to maintain other benefits during FMLA leave to ensure the employer's ability to provide the employee with equivalent benefits after return from leave without requalification.) For pension plans, unpaid FMLA leave is not a break in service but need not be treated as credited service for vesting and eligibility to participate.

Employee Reinstatement after Leave

Employees are entitled to return from their FMLA leave to the same or an equivalent position with similar benefits, pay, and other terms and conditions of employment and without loss of job seniority or any other status or benefits accrued prior to FMLA leave, provided those employees would still be employed if FMLA leave had not been taken. Thus, an employer may deny job restoration (a) when an employee's shift has been eliminated or if overtime has been decreased, (b) when an employee is hired for a specific term or for a discrete project and that term or project is over, or (c) when an employee has fraudulently obtained FMLA leave.

Under the FMLA, an employer is not required to create a new position or to place an employee in a different position if the employee is unable to perform the functions of his or her position at the conclusion of FMLA leave. (An employer may, however, have additional accommodation responsibilities under the Americans with Disabilities Act (ADA) or other state or federal statutes.) The employer is not required to restore an employee to an "equivalent" position when the employee was notified that he or she was to be replaced before the employee requested FMLA leave.

Certain "key employees" may be denied reinstatement if such denial is necessary to prevent substantial and grievous economic injury to the employer's operations. A key employee is a salaried eligible employee who is among the highest paid 10 percent of all employees at any covered worksite. The employer should advise the employee at the time of a request for, or commencement of, FMLA leave, or as soon thereafter as is practicable, that he or she qualifies as a key employee and that reinstatement may be denied if the employer decides that substantial and grievous economic injury to its operations would occur if the employee elected not to return to employment.

Notice Requirements for Employers

Covered employers are required to post a summary of FMLA rights and responsibilities in "conspicuous places" at all worksites. A model poster that has been approved by the U.S. Department of Labor is available from that department's Wage and Hour Division. Failure to post the notice may result in a civil money penalty not to exceed $100, and any employer who fails to post the notice cannot take adverse action against an employee, including denial of leave, for failing to furnish advance notice of the need to take leave.

If an employer has any written guidance to employees regarding benefits or leave rights (such as employee handbooks or manuals), the employer must include in those materials any information that describes employees' rights and responsibilities under the FMLA and any employer procedures for FMLA leaves. If an employer does not have these written materials, the employer must provide the FMLA information when the employee requests leave under the FMLA.

Within a reasonable time (1 or 2 business days) after an employee gives notice of the need for FMLA leave, the employer must provide specific information to the employee detailing the expectations and obligations regarding designation of leave, medical certification, substitution of paid leave, payment of employee health care premiums, fitness for duty certificate, status as key employee, right to job restoration, and potential liability for health insurance premiums. Employers may opt to include other information, such as a requirement for periodic reports on status and intent to return to work. This notice must be given to the employee no less often than the first time in each 6-month period that an employee gives notice of need for FMLA leave. Generally, employers who fail to provide the necessary notice may not take action against an employee for failure to comply with any of the provisions set forth in the notice.

CHAPTER 3

STATE AND LOCAL FAMILY AND MEDICAL LEAVES OF ABSENCE

In addition to the federal FMLA, many states, counties, and local jurisdictions have adopted FMLA laws that interact with the federal FMLA and, in some cases, supersede the federal act if the state or local law provides greater family and medical leave rights. California, Connecticut, the District of Columbia, Florida, Hawaii, Illinois, Maine, Minnesota, New Jersey, Oregon, Rhode Island, Vermont, Washington, and Wisconsin have state family and medical leave laws. Below are examples of a few FMLA laws enacted by different states, counties, and local jurisdictions. Employers should check to see whether there are relevant provisions in their individual state, county, or city.

State Laws

New Jersey

The New Jersey Family Leave Act (NJFLA) requires covered employers to provide certain employees with the opportunity to take temporary leaves of absence for up to 12 weeks in any 24-month period to care for newborn or adopted children or for seriously ill family members (including in-laws). The statute also guarantees that employees can return to their jobs, or to equivalent positions, upon the expiration of the leave. In addition, if both spouses work for the same employer, under the NJFLA, the employer cannot reduce the leave requirement to a combined total of 12 weeks of leave for both spouses (as is allowed under the federal FMLA). The NJFLA also specifies that employers must post notices describing employees' rights and obligations under the NJFLA and must "use other appropriate means to keep its employees so informed." The statute, as enacted, requires employers (a) to provide employees on family leave with the same health insurance coverage that would have been provided if the employees had continued working, and (b) to continue other benefits to the extent that they were provided to employees on other temporary leaves of absence. (These benefit continuation requirements were held to be preempted by the Employee Retirement Income Security Act. The state has, therefore, been enjoined from enforcing these provisions in the private sector.)

Connecticut

Connecticut's Family and Medical Leave Act (CFMLA) requires certain private employers to grant the following to workers who have been employed for 1 year or more: up to 16 weeks of unpaid leave of absence within any 2-year period for (a) the birth or adoption of a child; (b) the serious illness of a child, spouse, or parent; or (c) the worker's own serious illness. Under the CFMLA, employees are entitled to use the most advantageous combination of leave under the federal FMLA and the CFMLA laws. For example, an employee could take up to 16 weeks of family or medical leave in the year 1998 (under the Connecticut law) and then an additional 12 weeks of family or medical leave in the year 1999 (under the federal law).

District of Columbia

The District of Columbia Family and Medical Leave Act (DCFMLA) requires covered employers to provide eligible employees with the opportunity to take an unpaid family care leave of up to 16 weeks during a 24-month period in connection with a birth, adoption, or placement of a child for foster care or other permanent care, and the serious health condition of (a) a relative by blood, marriage, or legal custody; (b) a child living with the employee, who has assumed parental responsibility for the child; (c) a person sharing a mutual residence and committed to the relationship; or (d) the employee's own serious health condition. The statute guarantees that the employee, after being granted the leave request, may return to the same or a comparable position upon expiration of the leave.

The DCFMLA also requires employers to continue to allow employees taking a family care leave to participate in health plans, pension and retirement plans, and supplemental unemployment benefits plans to the same extent that those plans are provided to employees on other unpaid leaves of absence. Under the DCFMLA, employees are entitled to use the most advantageous combination of leave under the FMLA and DCFMLA. For example, an employee could take up to 16 weeks of family or medical leave in the year 1998 (under the District of Columbia's statute) and then an additional 12 weeks of family or medical leave in the year 1999 (under the federal statute).

California

The California Family Care Leave Act (CFCLA), recently amended, closely parallels the provisions of the FMLA. The CFCLA requires covered employers to provide eligible employees up to 12 weeks of unpaid leave in connection with the birth or adoption of a child or for a "serious health condition" of the employee or the employee's spouse, child, or parent. The statute guarantees that the employee, after being granted the leave requested, may return to the same or a comparable position upon expiration of the leave. Where differences in the FMLA and CFCLA exist, employers are required to comply with whichever law's provisions provide greater family and medical leave rights. Differences include the time allowed for pregnancy leave, which is discussed in chapter 4.

Florida

Florida's Family and Medical Leave Law applies to state employees who are in "career service." Those employees are entitled to leave in connection with the birth or adoption of a child, as well as for the care of a family member with a serious illness, including a child, parent, or spouse. Florida's statute defines career service employees as individuals working for the state, or for any committee, agency, or department of the state, who are not in "exempt positions." The exempt positions are many and include, among others, elected or appointed officials, employees of the state university system, temporary employees, employees in the governor's office, and most policy-making or managerial employees.

County and Local Laws

It is important that employers familiarize themselves with existing county and local ordinances that govern family and medical leave. For example, in December 1991, Miami–Dade County, Florida, approved a family leave ordinance that requires the following: all businesses that are in Miami–Dade County, as well as those businesses that do business with Miami–Dade County, and that employ 50 or more persons must provide up to 90 days of unpaid family leave during any 24-month period for the birth or adoption of a child, the care of a family member with a serious illness, or the employee's own serious illness. Those employers must maintain group health insurance coverage for the employee during the leave.

CHAPTER 4

PREGNANCY DISABILITY AND CHILD CARE LEAVE

Mandatory Federal Leave

In addition to family and medical leave of absence laws, Title VII of the Civil Rights Act of 1964, as amended by the Pregnancy Discrimination Act of 1978 (PDA), specifies that "women affected by pregnancy, childbirth, or related medical conditions shall be treated the same for all employment-related purposes, including receipt of benefits under fringe benefits programs, as other persons not so affected but similar in their ability or inability to work." The statute does not require that employers provide pregnancy disability or child care leaves per se, but only that these leaves be granted to the same extent and under the same conditions as other disability and nondisability leaves. Therefore, an employer's prior practices will play an important role in determining that employer's obligations, if any, to its pregnant employees who request a leave during their period of disability or for child care purposes.

Leave of absence for pregnancy-related disability must be provided on terms at least as favorable as those applied to other nonpregnancy disabilities. For example, an employer's leave of absence policy that limits pregnancy disability leave to 3 months, while no limit is placed on the duration of leave of absence for other illnesses or disabilities, violates Title VII.

Policies requiring employees to provide prompt notice of pregnancy, or requiring them to stop work at a particular point in their pregnancy, are generally unlawful.

An employer does not have to ignore the excessive absences or tardiness of a pregnant employee. Unless the pregnancy-related absence falls under the ADA's definition of disability or under the FMLA's provisions for intermittent leave (such as for prenatal examinations or for medical complications that render the employee unable to work), the employer can treat the absences the same way that it treats the similar behavior of nonpregnant employees. Under the PDA, an employer can hold a pregnant employee to the same quality performance standards as other employees and is not required to provide alternate duty as an accommodation.

The PDA does not require an employer to reinstate an employee on maternity leave. Instead, the employer must provide the same job protection afforded to other employees with nonpregnancy-related medical conditions. This policy differs from the reemployment requirements of the FMLA, discussed at length in chapter 2.

Under Title VII, employers that want to provide their employees with child care leave following the completion of the employees' disability must do so without regard to the employees' gender. The Equal Employment Opportunity Commission (EEOC) takes the position that Title VII "prohibits employers from establishing policies that treat male and female employees differently when such employees request time off to care for a newborn child." According to the EEOC, "[i]f an employer chooses to grant paid or unpaid leave to employees to allow for care and nurturing of a newborn child, the same leave must be provided to male and female employees." The EEOC's *Compliance Manual* advises that "the clearest safe harbor for employers ... is to separate the issue of pregnancy disability leave from the issue of parental leave. In this way, the employer may ensure that pregnancy disability leave is treated like all other forms of medical disability leave, while also establishing a single standard for parental leave that is applicable to males and females."

State Laws

Many states have enacted statutes, either under a family and medical leave law or a separate type of law, that provide additional protections to employees seeking leave for pregnancy or child care purposes.

California

For example, the California Fair Employment and Housing Act creates a separate pregnancy disability benefit under which an employer of five or more employees is required to provide up to 4 months of unpaid leave to any employee disabled on account of pregnancy, childbirth, or a related condition. This leave time is separate from, and in addition to, the 12 weeks of leave provided under the CFCLA, which largely parallels the FMLA. In fact, the U.S. Supreme

Court has held that Title VII, as amended by the PDA, did not preempt the California statute requiring employers to provide pregnancy leave of up to 4 months and reinstatement to employees disabled by pregnancy. The Supreme Court emphasized that the statute would allow benefits "to cover only the period of *actual physical disability*."

Florida

The Florida Family and Medical Leave Law provides that state "career service" employees are entitled to take up to 6 months of unpaid leave for the birth or adoption of a child.

New York

New York's adoption leave statute requires that, when a private employer or government agency permits an employee to take a leave of absence following the birth of his or her child, an adoptive parent of a young child is entitled to the same leave on the same terms following commencement of the parent-child relationship.

Maryland

The Maryland Human Relations Law specifically addresses the issue of pregnancy disability and provides that pregnancy disability shall be treated as temporary disability for all job-related purposes and that all policies and benefits that govern leaves shall treat pregnancy leaves in the same fashion as other disability leaves.

District of Columbia

The District of Columbia Human Rights Act provides that "[w]omen affected by pregnancy, childbirth, or related medical conditions shall be treated the same for all employment-related purposes, including receipt of benefits under fringe benefit programs, as other persons not so affected but similar in their ability or inability to work, and this requirement shall include, but not be limited to, a requirement that an employer must treat an employee temporarily unable to perform the functions of her job because of her pregnancy-related condition in the same manner as it treats other temporarily disabled employees."

CHAPTER 5

LEAVE UNDER THE AMERICANS WITH DISABILITIES ACT

Introduction

Unlike the laws discussed in chapters 2, 3, and 4, which are all laws that specifically require leaves of absence, the Americans with Disabilities Act of 1990 (ADA) is not a "leave" statute. Rather, it is a law that is intended to bring disabled workers *into* the workplace. The ADA does, however, require employers to consider leave as a means of satisfying their reasonable accommodation obligations under the law. This consideration comes as the last step in the analysis to determine whether an employee is entitled to an ADA leave of absence. The preliminary steps to determine employee eligibility are summarized next, followed by a discussion of ADA leave.

Employer Coverage

Beginning on July 26, 1994, Title I of the ADA covered employers that are engaged in an industry affecting commerce, and that have 15 or more employees for each working day in each of 20 or more calendar weeks in the current or preceding calendar year. (Before July 26, 1994, only employers with 25 or more employees were covered by Title I.) Temporary workers are considered employees and are protected by the ADA, as are agents of a covered employer. The United States, corporations wholly owned by the U.S. government, Indian tribes, and bona fide tax-exempt clubs with private membership are not covered by the ADA.

Individual Coverage

"Qualified individuals with disabilities" who apply to work for or who are employed by covered employers are entitled to coverage under the ADA.

The ADA defines a "qualified individual with a disability" as an individual with a disability who, with or without reasonable accommodation, can perform the essential functions of the employment position that such individual holds or desires. The ADA further requires that "consideration shall be given to the employer's judgment as to what functions of a job are essential."

Discrimination

Title I of the ADA provides that no employer "shall discriminate against a qualified individual with a disability because of the disability of such individual in regard to job application procedures, the hiring, advancement, or discharge of employees, employee compensation, job training, and other terms, conditions, and privileges of employment." The ADA defines "discriminate" to cover a wide spectrum of activities, including using standards or methods that have the effect of discriminating on the basis of disability, or that perpetuate discrimination of others subject to common administrative control and to not making reasonable accommodation unless it would impose undue hardship.

Disabilities Covered by the ADA

The ADA defines "disability" as a physical or mental impairment that substantially limits one or more of the major life activities of such individual, a record of such impairment, or being regarded as having such an impairment. Each sub-part of this definition has been defined in the regulations promulgated under the ADA.

Thus, the ADA regulations define "physical or mental impairment" as "any physiological disorder or condition, cosmetic disfigurement, or anatomical loss affecting one or more of the following body systems: neurological, musculoskeletal, special sense organs, respiratory (including speech organs), cardiovascular, reproductive, digestive, genito-urinary, hemic and lymphatic, skin, and endocrine; or any mental or psychological disorder, such as mental retardation, organic brain syndrome, emotional or mental illness, and specific learning disabilities."

"Substantially limits" is defined by the ADA regulations as unable to perform a major life activity that the average person in the general population can perform; or significantly restricted as to the condition, manner or duration under which the average person in the general population can perform that same major life activity.

"Major life activities" include such functions as "caring for oneself, performing manual tasks, walking, seeing, hearing, speaking, breathing, learning, and working." The EEOC's *Compliance Manual* has further expanded this list to include the mental and emotional processes of thinking, concentrating, and interacting with others.

To be disabled with regard to the major life activity of working, an individual must be substantially limited in the ability to perform either a class of jobs or a broad range of jobs in various classes as compared to the average person. It is not enough to be unable to perform a particular job.

Essential Functions

The ability to perform the essential functions of the job, with or without an accommodation, is the key ingredient for assessing whether the employee is covered by the ADA. "Essential functions" are defined in the ADA regulations as "[t]he fundamental job duties of the employment position the individual with a disability holds or desires. The term does not include the marginal functions of the position." Evidence of whether a particular function is essential includes, but is not limited to, the employer's judgment as to which jobs are essential; written job descriptions prepared before advertising or interviewing applicants for the job; the amount of time spent on the job performing the functions; the terms of a collective bargaining agreement, if any; the past work experience of previous incumbents in the job; and the current work experience of incumbents in similar jobs.

In the leave of absence context, it is recommended that employers consider listing "regular attendance" as an essential function in their job descriptions. The EEOC, however, takes the position that essential functions should be limited to functions that are performed after the employee shows up for work.

The "Reasonable Accommodation" Obligation

The ADA requires covered employers to provide "reasonable accommodations" to the known disabilities of qualified individuals. It is because reasonable accommodations may include granting temporary leave, as well as part-time or modified work schedules, that the ADA has been given its own chapter in this book. An employer is not, however, required to grant the specific accommodation requested by the employee, so long as the accommodation provided is reasonable. In addition, an employer is not obligated to provide a reasonable accommodation if doing so would constitute an "undue hardship" or pose a "direct threat."

An undue hardship is defined as "an action requiring significant difficulty or expense, when considered in light of the factors set forth...." Factors to be considered include "(a) the nature and cost of the accommodation needed under this Act; (b) the overall financial resources of the facility or facilities involved in the provision of the reasonable accommodation; (c) the number of persons employed at such facility; (d) the effect on expenses and resources, or the impact otherwise of such accommodation upon the operation of the facility; (e) the overall financial resources of the covered entity; (f) the overall size of the business of a covered entity with respect to the number of its employees; (g) the number, type, and location of its facilities; (h) the type of operation or operations of the covered entity, including the composition, structure, and functions of the workforce of such entity; and (i) the geographic separateness, administrative, and fiscal relationship of the facility or facilities in question to the covered entity."

The regulations provide that to determine the nature and cost of an accommodation, the employer must take into account the availability of tax credits and deductions and/or outside funding. In addition, the regulations include as an additional factor "[t]he impact of an accommodation upon the operation of the facility, including the impact on the ability of other employees to perform their duties and the impact on the facility's ability to conduct business."

Although an employer probably need not explore the "direct threat" defense to a request for a leave of absence as a reasonable accommodation, it should be noted that under the ADA a direct threat is "a significant risk to the health or safety of others that cannot be eliminated by reasonable accommodation." The regulations add that the term means "a significant risk of substantial harm to the individual or others that cannot be eliminated or reduced by reasonable accommodation."

Leave as a Reasonable Accommodation

The EEOC requires employers to consider unpaid leaves as a form of reasonable accommodation. Therefore, employers must analyze whether an employee is a qualified individual with a disability to determine whether (and to what extent) they are required to provide that employee with a leave under the ADA.

Employers should be aware that temporary impairments are not considered disabilities under the ADA. Thus, an employee who requests a leave of absence because of a temporary condition, such as a broken leg, is not entitled to an accommodation under the ADA for leave or other purposes.

An employee is entitled to an effective accommodation, not necessarily the best accommodation available. The employer and the employee should consider whether reasonable accommodations other than leaves are available, such as accommodations within the job (for example, special equipment, extended break periods, modified work schedule) that will permit the employee to perform the essential functions of the job, or such as a transfer to a vacant position.

If the employee seeking an ADA leave of absence also has a serious health condition and is otherwise qualified, the employer should consider the employee's rights under the FMLA when evaluating the employee's leave request for disability reasons. In many respects, an employee's rights with respect to leave are greater, and an employer's rights more restricted, under the FMLA.

The Length of the ADA Leave

If an employee is disabled and requires (and requests) a leave because of a disability, the employer must consider whether to provide a leave and the length of that leave. To make this determination, the employer must keep two principles in mind. First, an employer is not required by the ADA to provide a leave if the leave, or the length of the leave, would constitute an undue hardship for the employer. While there is no hard and fast rule on how much leave constitutes an undue hardship, the reported cases so far have sided with the employers when 1-year leave of absence requests have been denied. In fact, one court has ruled that an employer did not violate the ADA because an employee's request for additional leave time after a 7-month leave was unreasonable. Second, an employer is not required by the ADA to provide indefinite leaves. Because an individual requiring an indefinite leave would not be a qualified individual with a disability, an employer may deny a request that is supported by a doctor's note that does not specify a date of return.

An employer may be required to provide additional leave as a reasonable accommodation—even beyond leave that is provided by the employer's existing policies. In other words, "wooden" leave policy deadlines may have to be extended in appropriate circumstances. But according to one court, it is not discriminatory to terminate an employee who failed to return to work upon the expiration of an approved leave, pursuant to the employer's established medical leave policy, because the employee did not ask for additional leave before the expiration of the approved leave.

Employers should also be aware that courts treat the employer's duty to provide reasonable accommodation as a continuing one and not one exhausted by a single effort. For example, an employer that had already provided paid disability leave for a year to a long-term employee who had a mental breakdown was then required to allow the employee to return to work part-time for 4 weeks as a reasonable accommodation for his disability.

In the context of employee leaves, employers must consider transfers to vacant positions at the following points: when the employee first requests the leave, at any point during the leave when the employee seeks to return to work in a different position, or at the end of the leave period. The duty to consider transfers arises from the fact that the ADA requires employers to consider reassignment to a vacant position as a form of reasonable accommodation. However, employers are required to re-assign an employee to a vacant position only if the employee can perform the essential functions of the vacant position with or without a reasonable accommodation.

As a general matter, an employer does not have to provide an accommodation unless one is requested. Thus, an employer could argue that it is not required to consider granting a leave or transferring an employee to a vacant position as a reasonable accommodation unless the employee requests a leave or a transfer. However, once an employee with a disability makes a request for an accommodation, such as a request for a leave, an employer is obligated to engage in an "interactive process" to determine an appropriate accommodation.

Excessive Absenteeism

Most courts that have considered the issue of absenteeism under either the ADA or the Rehabilitation Act have held that an employee who is excessively absent is not a qualified individual with a disability because regular attendance is an essential function of virtually every job. Several courts have also held that an employer cannot accommodate unpredictable or sporadic absenteeism. For a limited number of jobs, however, regular attendance at work may not be an essential function of the job.

Leaves Relating to Substance or Alcohol Abuse

An individual who has successfully completed a drug rehabilitation program and is no longer using illegal drugs, or who has otherwise been successfully rehabilitated and is not currently using illegal drugs, is protected as an individual with a "disability" under the ADA. Similarly, an individual who is participating in a rehabilitation program and is no longer engaging in use of illegal drugs is protected by the ADA.

Employers may be faced with requests by employees for leaves of absences to attend drug or alcohol treatment programs. Because a "current" illegal user of drugs is not an "individual with a disability" under the ADA, a request from a current user may be denied. The problem, however, is that what constitutes a "current" illegal user of drugs is not clearly defined. According to the EEOC's *Technical Assistance Manual,* "[c]urrent drug use means that the illegal use of drugs occurred recently enough to justify an employer's reasonable belief that involvement with drugs is an on-going problem. It is not limited to the day of use, or recent weeks or days, in terms of an employment action. It is determined on a case-by-case basis." Therefore, as a practical matter, if an employer catches an employee using drugs and decides to fire him or her, the employee cannot save his or her job by making a request to go to a rehabilitation clinic right before (or after) the termination decision is announced.

Moreover, according to the EEOC, "[i]f an individual tests positive on a test for the illegal use of drugs, the individual will be considered a current drug user under the ADA." Therefore, an employee who tests positive for illegal drug use is not entitled to a leave to attend a drug treatment program as a reasonable accommodation. Once an employee enters a program, the employee would be an individual participating in a rehabilitation program and would be protected by the ADA provided that he or she is no longer using illegal drugs. But an employee would lose that protection if the employee resumed illegal drug use after the employer had permitted the employee to enter a drug treatment program.

A recovering drug addict who is not currently using drugs illegally may, however, be entitled to an accommodation in work schedule to attend ongoing self-help programs, such as Narcotics Anonymous. Covered employers are entitled to seek reasonable assurances that no illegal drug use is occurring or has occurred recently, which would make continuing use a real and ongoing problem.

Alcoholism is a disability under the ADA. Unlike illegal drug use, however, current use of alcohol does not disqualify an individual from protection under the ADA; that is an alcoholic who currently uses alcohol may be a qualified individual with a disability. According to the EEOC's *Technical Assistance Manual*, an employer may discipline, discharge, or deny employment to an alcoholic whose use of alcohol adversely affects job performance or conduct to the extent the individual is not "qualified." Thus, an alcoholic who is often late for work or unable to perform the responsibilities of his or her position may be disciplined on the basis of the poor performance and conduct (but not more severely than other employees with similar poor performance and conduct).

Under the ADA, employers will likely be required to afford employees afflicted with alcoholism with leaves of absence as a reasonable accommodation to attend alcohol treatment programs. For example, one court has found that an employer could have reasonably accommodated an employee by providing a leave of absence when the employee entered a 28-day inpatient program to treat alcoholism. Recovering alcoholics may also be entitled to an accommodation in work schedule to attend ongoing self-help programs such as Alcoholics Anonymous.

A cautionary note should be sounded for employers who want to "do the right thing" and offer employees an option to either take a leave of absence to enroll in a rehabilitation program or be terminated for drinking or intoxication during working hours. At least one appellate court has found that this option, which included a threat of termination, may be illegal discrimination on the basis of the perceived disability caused by alcoholism. If proven, the employer would be liable for reinstatement, back pay, and the other ADA remedies.

CHAPTER 6

WORKERS' COMPENSATION LEAVES

Coping with Return-to-Work Issues

The purpose of state workers' compensation laws is to provide a system for giving employees a prompt and fair settlement of their claims against employers for industrial injuries and illnesses. As a general rule, workers' compensation laws cover practically all business entities, sometimes even those with as few as one or two employees. Although subject to certain exceptions, states can protect employees who work in a trade, business, or occupation carried on by the employer for pecuniary gain.

While all state workers' compensation laws have this common purpose, their methods and means of accomplishing that purpose are quite individualized. Questions concerning leaves may be answered differently under one law than under others. Therefore, it is necessary to check the law in the jurisdiction where the injury occurred. The following generalizations should help to facilitate a specific state law inquiry.

Most state workers' compensation laws do not require leaves of absence as a result of occupational injuries. In addition, workers' compensation laws generally do not require reinstatement, provided that the reason for denial of reinstatement and/or the termination of employment is not in retaliation for filing a workers' compensation claim. In other words, an industrial injury is generally not a guarantee of job protection. Conversely, an employer must treat a request for leave in conjunction with an injury or illness that could result, or has resulted, in workers' compensation benefits no less favorably than the employer would treat a request for a leave of absence for any other illness or injury. Otherwise, the denial of the leave could be deemed unlawful retaliation under the retaliation provisions of most state laws.

CHAPTER 7

THE INTERPLAY AMONG THE ADA, FMLA, AND WORKERS' COMPENSATION: ANSWERS TO PRACTICAL, DIFFICULT LEAVE ISSUES

Employers are confronted by a thicket of complex and often seemingly inconsistent laws and regulations when an employee asks for time off because of a medical condition. Understandably so—the ADA, the FMLA, and state workers' compensation statutes have created considerable confusion for employers who are confronted with such requests. To begin with, the laws have different roots: the ADA is a civil rights–oriented antidiscrimination law, the FMLA is essentially a labor standard and leave law, and workers' compensation law is a no-fault insurance law. At the same time, employers must be aware of areas of substantial overlap as they try to manage their compliance with these laws. Employers, who may be covered by some, all, or none of the statutes, must be aware of the different, and often overlapping, obligations both when developing leave policies and when responding to leave requests.

ADA and FMLA

Two of the most complicated sources of law in the legal thicket are the ADA and the FMLA, which create overlapping obligations for an employer faced with a leave request. At a minimum, human resources professionals should be aware that ADA and FMLA issues lurk at the roots of most leave issues. Failure to consider the implications of both statutes will result in employers finding themselves entangled in legal issues and watching their legal exposure grow.

Eligibility and Amount of Leave

Employees may be entitled to leave under both the FMLA and the ADA. Because the FMLA's leave requirements are more specific and technical, the employer should look first to the FMLA when an employee requests time off for a medical condition. As more fully discussed in chapter 2, assuming that an employee with a serious health condition is eligible for FMLA leave, the length of the leave is specifically prescribed by the statute—12 workweeks of unpaid leave (with continued health coverage) that can be taken in a continuous block of time, intermittently, or on a reduced work schedule.

If an employee does not qualify for FMLA leave, or when—as frequently happens—an employee on FMLA leave requests additional leave beyond the 12 weeks required by FMLA, the employer may be obligated under the ADA to provide leave to a disabled employee as a reasonable accommodation, absent undue hardship. As discussed in chapter 5, before granting leave under the ADA, an employer should always consider whether an employee has a disability under the ADA, and whether the leave requested would be reasonable and would not impose an undue hardship on the business.

Unlike the FMLA, the ADA provides no maximum amount of leave—nor does it define what length of leave is reasonable or an undue hardship. As with many issues under the ADA, employers must consider each request for leave on a case-by-case basis. The following guidelines, however, may be helpful.

Generally, a short-term leave would likely be considered reasonable. However, at least one court has held that 1 year's leave is clearly too long. Also, an employer is not required to grant an indefinite leave under the ADA. Practically speaking, employers should request that employees on ADA leave provide them with specific, reasonable return-to-work dates. While there may be circumstances in which an employer should consider extending an agreed-upon return-to-work date (for example, if an employee takes longer to recuperate than was initially anticipated), fixing a return-to-work date provides the employer with a degree of control over the length of the leave and allows the employer to plan for the eventual return of the employee.

Permissible Medical Information and Documentation Requests

Determining the types of information and documentation that an employer may seek will depend on which statute covers the employee's leave request. Under the ADA, the employer may make inquiries that are job related and consistent with business necessity when addressing an employee's disabilities. Reasonable inquiries (including reasonable requests for medical documentation) and medical exams of a disabled employee (by a physician of the employer's choosing) may be required to determine if an employee requesting leave is disabled under the ADA and what accommodation might be necessary. The ADA requires that medical information relating to a person's disability or occupational injury be maintained on separate forms and in separate personnel files. An employer must keep a person's medical information confidential, even if that person is no longer an applicant or employee.

According to the EEOC, medical inquiries specifically permitted by the FMLA are also permissible under the ADA because they are by definition job related and consistent with business necessity. The converse, however, is not true. The FMLA is more restrictive than the ADA with respect to the quantity of information that may be obtained and the methods that may be used to obtain the information.

Under the FMLA, the employer initially may require a medical certification that is from the employee's health care provider and that provides only information contained on the Certification of Health Care Provider form prescribed by the U.S. Department of Labor. An employer cannot ask for more information than that which the Department of Labor permits an employer to obtain. This restriction is true even if the employee requesting FMLA leave also happens to be disabled within the meaning of the ADA. Accordingly, if the employee is covered by both the ADA and the FMLA, employers, as a rule of thumb, should follow the FMLA medical certification requirements for leave requests.

Unlike with the ADA, an employer faced with an FMLA request cannot request additional information from a health care provider to determine whether FMLA leave is required even if the employer believes that the additional information would otherwise be job related and consistent with business necessity. Rather, the FMLA regulations specifically detail the procedure for obtaining and verifying medical certification. Initially, the employer may, with the employee's consent, have an independent health care provider contact the employee's health care provider to authenticate and/or clarify the certification. If further inquiry is desired, the FMLA requires that the employer have an independent health care provider examine the employee (at the employer's expense). If the second health care provider does not certify the employee's serious health condition, a third health care provider, chosen by the first two, can examine the employee (at the employer's expense) and can provide a third and binding opinion. If the FMLA applies to an employee's leave request, deviation from these procedures will expose an employer to potential liability.

Because FMLA is unpaid leave, the FMLA's restrictions on the method and means of verifying illness do not interfere with an employer's right to impose additional requirements on employees who are entitled to FMLA but who also seek payment under the employer's paid sick leave policy. Therefore, as long as an employer requests the same medical verification from all employees who want to be paid for their absence that was caused by illness, then the employer may, for example, require a "doctor's note" containing information that is not included on the Department of Labor's Certification of Health Care Provider Form and is otherwise not available from an employee whose FMLA is unpaid.

Employee Transfers

The FMLA allows an employer to temporarily transfer an employee to another position to accommodate a reduced or intermittent schedule. Although the temporary transfer position need not have the same duties as the original position, the employer must comport with any obligations due under any collective bargaining agreements, and the employee continues to be entitled to pay and benefits equivalent to those that were received by the employee before the transfer.

The ADA, however, is much more restrictive than the FMLA; ADA permits transfers of employees under only two circumstances. Employers are allowed to make a transfer only if employees are incapable of performing the essential functions of their present position and if accommodations were not possible in the present position. A transfer is also permitted if an accommodation in an employee's present position would cause an undue hardship. Unlike the FMLA, an employer may reduce pay if the new position carries a lower salary and may refuse to continue benefits for a disabled employee who is transferred to a part-time position, provided that the employer does not ordinarily maintain those benefits for other similarly situated part-time workers.

Reinstatement Issues

The FMLA requires that the employee returning from leave be given the same position or one equivalent to the one held before a leave. Although the employer cannot discriminate against the employee on the basis of the leave request, the FMLA does not require the employer to make any other accommodations for the returning employee, including modifications to the job or transfer to another available position.

If, however, the employee is disabled under the ADA at the time of his or her return to work, that employee will be entitled to a reasonable accommodation under the ADA, absent an undue hardship. Thus, a returning disabled employee may be entitled to modifications in the manner in which the job is done, or even the elimination of non-essential functions of the job that he or she cannot perform because of a disability. And if the employer cannot accommodate the employee within the existing job, the employer must consider transferring the employee to a vacant position for which he or she is qualified as a reasonable accommodation.

Thus, even though an employer's obligations under the FMLA conclude when the employee returns to the same or a substantially equivalent position, the human resources professional must always consider whether additional ADA considerations are implicated in the return to work of a disabled employee.

Intermittent Leave or Reduced Schedule Issues

The FMLA allows employees to take leave on an intermittent basis where medically necessary because of their own serious health condition or the serious health condition of a child, spouse, or parent. Intermittent leave may include leave periods of from 1 hour or more to several weeks. Because absenteeism is protected for up to 12 workweeks if it is the result of a serious health condition, it is possible for an employee to take intermittent FMLA leave (such as for 1 day per week during a 12-month period) and to never exhaust his or her entitlement to FMLA leave. Employers are prohibited from disciplining or discharging employees who take intermittent FMLA leave.

Unlike the FMLA, however, the ADA permits nondiscriminatory employment actions that are based on excessive or sporadic absenteeism. Therefore, employers should determine whether the leave time is FMLA protected before taking action against an employee for absences.

No-Fault Policies

An FMLA absence cannot be counted as an "occasion of absence" under the "no-fault" attendance policies that exist in many companies. As a result, employers with "no-fault" attendance policies must ensure that FMLA-protected absences are not counted for the purposes of their "no-fault" policies. To help an employer ensure that FMLA-protected absences are not improperly counted, it is important to educate individuals who are responsible for discipline about the FMLA, and to centralize the no-fault and FMLA record-keeping functions so that the same group of individuals administers both policies.

Because the FMLA has interfered with the effectiveness of "no-fault" policies, one frequently asked question is how an employer can "get around" the FMLA's prohibition against counting FMLA absences under a "no-fault" policy. To date, the answer remains that it cannot be done per se, although more and more employers are beginning to challenge the FMLA eligibility of employees. An increasing number of employers question an employee's original certification by sending the employee to a second (and, if necessary, a third) health care provider. At the same time, employers are hiring more investigators to determine whether an employee has made a fraudulent claim (such as an employee who "can't" come to work because of a serious health condition but is videotaped on the golf course).

While the increased exercise of an employer's rights under the FMLA may not improve attendance in all cases, the diminished effectiveness of "no-fault" policies may improve as dubious medical claims are deterred.

FMLA and Workers' Compensation

Employer Management Issues

No leave resulting from a workers' compensation injury or illness is generally required under most workers' compensation statutes, but if the injury or illness also constitutes a serious health condition, leave may be required under the FMLA. Thus, an employee who suffers from a "serious health condition" caused by a work-related injury is entitled to workers' compensation benefits and to a continuation of benefits under the FMLA.

Workers' compensation laws allow an employer to offer an employee a light duty assignment, and the employee is permitted, but not required, to accept the assignment (although refusal of a light duty assignment generally will result in a decrease of workers' compensation benefits). For an employee who is also FMLA eligible, the employer may not require the employee to work in a light duty assignment in lieu of FMLA leave. The FMLA-eligible employee may decline the employer's offer of a light duty job and may remain on unpaid FMLA leave until that employee's 12-week entitlement runs out. If the employee loses workers' compensation payments as a result, the employee may substitute qualifying paid vacation, personal, or sick leave for unpaid leave. If the employee accepts a light duty position, the employee is entitled to return to the same or an equivalent position until the 12-week entitlement (including FMLA leave and the period in a light duty job) runs out. The period of time employed in a light duty assignment cannot count, however, against the employee's 12-week entitlement to FMLA leave.

In some states, an employee taking FMLA leave to care for a family member who has suffered a workers' compensation injury severe enough to justify nursing care may be entitled to payment from the family member's employer.

In addition, unlike under the FMLA, some states permit employers with a "no-fault" leave policy to consider workers' compensation absences when counting occasions of absence under the policy.

ADA and Workers' Compensation

On September 3, 1996, the EEOC provided general guidance on the interaction between Title I of the ADA and state workers' compensation laws. That guidance is summarized below.

Defining Disability

An employee with an occupational injury may have a "disability" as defined by workers' compensation law but may not meet any of the three definitions of a "disability" under the ADA.

First, an employee may have an occupational impairment, but the impairment may not be severe enough to substantially limit a major life activity (for example, it may be only temporary, may be nonchronic, or may have little or no long-term impact).

Second, an employee who has filed a workers' compensation claim might not necessarily be considered to have a "record of" a disability under the ADA.

Third, an employee with an occupational injury might not necessarily be "regarded as" having a disability under the ADA. A person with an occupational injury is "regarded as" having a disability under the ADA if she or he (a) has an impairment that does not substantially limit a major life activity but is treated by an employer as if it were substantially limiting, (b) has an impairment that substantially limits a major life activity because of the attitude of others toward the impairment, or (c) has no impairment but it treated as having a substantially limiting impairment.

Disability-Related Questions and Examinations

Generally speaking, workers' compensation laws do not limit an employer's right to ask applicants questions about their workers' compensation history or to require applicants and employees to submit to medical examinations.

In contrast, the ADA limits the extent to which an employer may ask disability-related questions or may require medical examinations that are related to workers' compensation claims and occupational injuries. Under the ADA, employers may ask questions about an applicant's prior workers' compensation claims or occupational injuries only after they have extended a conditional offer of employment and only if they ask the same questions of all entering employees in a job category. Likewise, an employer may require an applicant to undergo a medical examination in order to obtain information about prior occupational injuries only after it has extended a conditional offer of employment and only if it requires medical examinations of all entering employees in a job category. For employees who have accepted a conditional offer of employment and for existing employees, an employer may ask disability-related questions or may require a medical examination of an employee who experiences an occupational injury or who seeks to return to the job following an occupational injury. The questions or examinations must not exceed the scope of the specific occupational injury and its effect on the employee's ability, with or without reasonable accommodation, to perform essential job functions or to work without posing a direct threat. To ascertain the extent of its workers' compensation liability, an employer may also ask disability-related questions or require a medical examination of an employee with an occupational injury.

Reasonable Accommodations

The ADA does not require that employers provide reasonable accommodations to employees with occupational injuries that do not qualify as "disabilities" under the ADA.

The ADA does require, however, that employers provide reasonable accommodations to employees with occupational injuries that also qualify as "disabilities" under the ADA. An employer may not discharge an employee who is temporarily unable to work because of a disability-related occupational injury where providing leave as a reasonable accommodation would not impose an undue hardship. As a reasonable accommodation, an employer must reallocate the marginal job duties of an employee with a disability-related occupational injury.

An employer may not reassign an employee with a disability-related occupational injury to a different position without first trying to accommodate the employee in the position held at the time of injury. If an employee can no longer perform the essential functions of the original position because of a disability-related occupational injury, or if it would be an undue hardship to accommodate the employee in that position, then the employee must be assigned to an equivalent position for which he or she is qualified.

If no equivalent position is available, the employee must be reassigned to a lower-level vacant position. An employer need not create a new position or "bump" another employee to reassign an employee with a disability-related occupational injury. An employer may not satisfy its obligation to provide reasonable accommodation by placing an employee with a disability-related occupational injury in a workers' compensation vocational rehabilitation service. An employer may make workplace modifications beyond what is required by the ADA in an effort to offset workers' compensation costs. If an employee with a disability-related occupational injury requests reasonable accommodation, the employer may require reasonable documentation of that employee's entitlement to reasonable accommodation.

Returning to Work

Under the ADA, an employer may not require that an employee with a disability-related occupational injury be able to return to "full duty" before allowing him or her to return to work. An employer may not refuse to return an employee to work because it assumes the employee's disability-related occupational injury creates an increased risk of future injuries and increased workers' compensation costs. An employer may, however, refuse to allow an employee to return to work if it can show that the employee would pose a "direct threat." The EEOC's *Enforcement Guidance* provides the following example: C, a typist, breaks his wrist while trying to move heavy office equipment. C is unable to work for 6 weeks and receives workers' compensation. C's wrist heals and his physician indicates there is little risk that repetitive motion will damage C's wrist. C's employer may not refuse his request to return to work because the employer fears that repetitive motion will cause serious and permanent reinjury.

An employer may not refuse to return an employee to work because that employee's disability-related occupational injury is considered a "permanent" or "total" disability under workers' compensation law. The EEOC's *Enforcement Guidance* provides the following example: An employee who loses vision in both eyes or the use of both arms may have a "permanent disability" for workers' compensation purposes but may still be able to work.

An employee with a disability-related occupational injury is entitled to return to his or her original position, unless the employer demonstrates that for the employee to do so would create an undue hardship.

Reassignment and Transfer

Under workers' compensation laws, if an ill or injured employee is returned to work by transfer or reassignment, his or her wage-loss compensation may be reduced either in part or in full. Moreover, if an employee refuses available work that can be done within the employee's restrictions, the employer may move to terminate or modify wage-loss benefits.

But if the workers' compensation injury or illness is also an ADA disability, the ADA permits transfer of an employee only (a) if the employee is incapable of performing the essential functions of his or her present position and an accommodation is impossible in the present position, or (b) if an accommodation in the employee's present position would cause an undue hardship. In general, reassignment applies only to current employees and not to applicants, and it is used sparingly by employers as a last resort. An employer may refuse to continue benefits for a disabled employee who is transferred to a part-time position, provided that the employer does not ordinarily maintain those benefits for other part-time workers.

Light Duty Positions

"Light duty" is defined as a position created specifically for the purpose of providing work for employees who are unable to perform some or all of their normal duties. The ADA neither requires nor prohibits the creation of light duty positions for employees who have been injured on the job. According to the EEOC, if an employer creates light duty positions for employees with occupational injuries, it must also offer light duty positions as reasonable accommodation to disabled employees who were not injured on the job.

If an employee is returned to work with no reduction in wages, that employee will cease receiving workers' compensation benefits for lost wages. This situation will not affect medical payments for job-related injuries or illness, nor will it affect scheduled awards that compensate the employee for the permanent loss of use of a body part, regardless of the impact of that loss on wage earning capacity.

Preexisting Conditions

Under the ADA, employers may not discriminate against a job applicant or employee who has preexisting conditions or disabilities, so long as that person can perform the essential job functions with or without reasonable accommodation. Except in special circumstances (such as an applicant with an obvious disability), questions regarding preexisting conditions or disabilities are permitted only after a conditional offer of employment is made, and may consist only of inquiries into an employee's ability to perform job functions. This restriction increases the risk that an employer will hire an individual who has a greater need for workers' compensation benefits.

Several states have addressed this potential for added liability by establishing second injury funds, which limit the amount of the second employer's liability for workers' compensation benefits to an employee who had a preexisting condition unrelated to the current employment. Employers who ask about preexisting conditions to take advantage of these special funds should do so only after a conditional offer has been made.

Disability Benefits

One common problem that arises for employers under the ADA and workers' compensation statutes is whether employees' claims that are in their applications for workers' compensation or other disability benefits and that describe their ability or inability to work will determine whether the employees are disabled according to definitions of the ADA. Recent EEOC guidance maintains that "... representations about the ability to work made in the course of applying for the Social Security, workers' compensation, disability insurance, and other disability benefits do not bar the filing of an ADA claim." While the guidance is not binding in courts, EEOC investigators must use several factors to assess whether the representations that an employee has made when applying for disability benefits will determine whether that employee is also a qualified individual with a disability under the ADA.

CHAPTER 8

MILITARY LEAVES OF ABSENCE

When it comes to ranking the impact of federal leave laws on the workplace, the two laws governing military leaves are at or near the bottom. Unless, of course, a war breaks out. Then the dust comes off the military leave policies, and employment lawyers who claim an "expertise" in this arcane area become "hot items" on television news programs. If you do not make leave decisions based on what you hear and see on television, here's what you need to know.

USERRA

The Uniform Services Employment and Reemployment Rights Act of 1994 (USERRA) regulates military leave. It provides benefits and reemployment rights to employees who are temporarily absent from civilian employment because of noncareer obligations to a "uniformed service." (USERRA replaced the Veterans' Reemployment Rights Law of 1940.)

To understand USERRA, one must understand that the statutory purpose of USERRA is "to encourage noncareer service in the Uniformed Services by eliminating or minimizing the disadvantages to civilian careers and employment which can result from such service; [and] to minimize the disruption to the lives of persons performing service in the Uniformed Services by providing for the prompt reemployment of such persons upon their completion of service under honorable conditions."

Covered Employers

Surprising as it may seem, USERRA has broader applications than any federal law previously discussed. In short, USERRA applies to *all* employers, including state and federal governments. The term "employer" includes any person, institution, organization, or other entity that pays a salary or wages for work performed by an individual. What makes USERRA so far-reaching are the facts that there is no requirement that an employer be engaged in interstate commerce and no minimum number of employees required for an employer to be covered.

Covered Employees

There are no employee eligibility requirements in USERRA. Any person working for an employer is an employee covered by the USERRA. There is no minimum service requirement, and the USERRA provisions that protect against discrimination and retaliation apply to employment applicants as well as to individuals who are not members of the uniformed services.

Covered Military Services

USERRA guarantees the employment rights of service persons in most voluntary and involuntary service categories, including the members of the U.S. Army, Navy, Air Force, Marines, and Coast Guard, as well as members of the National Guard, Reserves, or Public Health Service. Any other category of "uniformed services" designated by the President during a war or emergency is also entitled to coverage.

Benefit Entitlement and Reemployment Rights

Although every employer, every employee, and every military branch is covered, any employee absent from work as a result of military service must satisfy four requirements to be entitled to the benefits and reemployment rights under USERRA.

First, the employee, or an appropriate military officer, is required to give written or verbal advance notice to the employer that he or she will be absent from the job because of military service or training. Although the USERRA does not set an exact time frame for which advance notice must be given, Congress indicated that an employee should make every effort when possible to give timely notice, and that giving notice at the last minute—when it could have been given earlier but was unjustifiably not given—should be viewed unfavorably.

Second, the cumulative length of absence because of military service cannot exceed 5 years, although only the absences from the employer with whom the employee seeks reemployment are cumulated.

Military Leaves of Absence

Third, the employee must receive an honorable release from military service, and fourth, the employee is required to submit an application for reemployment within a reasonable amount of time.

The employees who meet these eligibility criteria not only are entitled to a military leave of absence, but also must acquire certain health, pension, reinstatement, and other benefit considerations described below. Employers must provide eligible service persons with COBRA-like health benefit continuation for up to 18 months during their military service. (But if other employees are expected to pay their share of costs for benefits during leave, employees who are absent for military duty may be required to contribute their share.) For employees on a military leave of absence under USERRA, most health plans are covered, including group health plans, insured health coverage, self-funded employer health plans, health maintenance organizations, preferred provider organizations, and health care flexible spending accounts.

While on leave, employees must also receive pension benefit plan protection, which means that their time in the uniformed service must be considered as service with the employer for both vesting and benefit accrual purposes, provided that the employee is reemployed within the prescribed time period allowed by USERRA.

The rules for benefits other than health and pension are not as specific. As a rule of thumb, an employee who is absent for military duty is entitled to the same benefits given to other employees with similar salary levels and seniority who take a leave of absence for nonmilitary reasons. (A waiver of benefits can occur when an employee knowingly provides written notice of an intent not to return to employment following the end of military service.)

Under USERRA's "escalator" method, upon reemployment, employees must return to the seniority and benefits level where they would have been had they not taken military leave. For leave that lasts for fewer than 91 days, the employer must place returning individuals in the positions they would be in if they had been continuously employed. For military service of more than 90 days, the employer must treat the employee as if continuous employment had occurred, or must place the employee in a new position—provided the individual is qualified—with similar seniority, status, and pay as the prior position. If an employee is not qualified for either position, and if reasonable efforts have been made, an employer may place the employee in any other position of lesser status and pay.

Under certain limited circumstances, an employer is not required to reemploy an individual who has returned from military leave, including the following: (a) changed circumstances make reemployment impossible or unreasonable; (b) reemployment of a disabled individual or of one who is no longer qualified to perform his or her job would create an undue hardship on the employer; or (c) the employment was for a brief, nonrecurrent period and there was no expectation that employment would continue indefinitely for a significant period of time.

Reemployment rights must also be extended to employees who have service-related disabilities and who can be reasonably accommodated.

Reapplication Requirements for Employment upon Return

As previously stated, an employee who returns from military leave must submit an application for reemployment or must report to the place of employment. The deadline by which an employee must make an application or report for reemployment is tied to the length of the intervening military service. Under USERRA, if the military service is for fewer than 31 days, an employee satisfies the requirement by reporting to the place of employment not later than the "beginning of the first full regularly scheduled working period on the first full calendar day following completion of service and expiration of 8 hours after time for safe transportation back to his or her residence." An employer must give the returning employee a reasonable amount of time to rest and to travel to the place of employment. If the length of service is more than 30 days but fewer than 181 days, an employee must submit an application for reemployment no later than 14 days after the end of military service. If unable to meet this deadline through no fault of his or her own, the employee must submit the application on the next calendar day that submission becomes possible. For military service that lasts longer than 180 days, an application for reemployment must be submitted to the employer no later than 90 days after the conclusion of service. These deadlines for reapplication can, however, be extended for up to 2 years for an employee who is hospitalized or recovering from an injury that occurred during the military service.

An employee who fails to meet the applicable deadline does not automatically forfeit reemployment. Instead, the employee is subject to any disciplinary policies that pertain to absence from work and that are maintained by the employer. As a requirement for reemployment, an employee whose military leave was for more than 30 days must comply with an employer's request for documentation to demonstrate that the application for reemployment was timely, that the combined military leave does not exceed 5 years, or that the service ended under honorable circumstances.

Military Leave Policies

Most employers who have written military leave policies use the generic, plain vanilla format and state simply that they will comply with their legal obligations regarding military leave. Those employers should be warned, however, that employers who do not develop a specific written policy for employees on military leave may be required to provide the same nonstatutory benefits that are given to employees under the employers' FMLA policies. Therefore, an employer will be required to provide to employees on military leave all of the benefits given to its employees on FMLA leave, in addition to the benefits provided by USERRA.

VEVRA

In developing military leave policies, employers must also take into account the Vietnam Era Veterans' Readjustment Assistance Act of 1974 (VEVRA).

VEVRA guarantees the employment rights of veterans and of members of the Reserves and the National Guard. Under this statute, veterans seeking reemployment must be returned to positions of like seniority, status, and pay. The statute also limits an employer's ability to discharge covered employees. In addition, the law contains a general prohibition of discrimination against veterans, reservists, and members of the National Guard. As a result, it is unlawful to discharge or to deny any promotion to reservists because of their military obligations.

State Laws

A final source of rights of employees who seek military leave can be found in the various state laws that guarantee the employment rights of military personnel and, in some cases, provide for additional benefits for these employees. In addition, many state statutes require that public service employers pay their employees for a certain length of time during their leaves of absence.

Florida

Under Florida's Military Affairs and Related Matters statute, "any person who seeks or holds an employment position must not be denied employment or retention in employment, or any promotion or advantage of employment, because of any obligation as a member of a reserve component of the Armed Forces." Any officer or employee of the state of Florida, of any county of the state, or of any municipality or political subdivision of the state who is a member of the Florida National Guard is entitled to leave of absence from his or her respective employment duties, without loss of pay, time, or efficiency rating, on all days during which he or she is engaged in active state duty. Leave of absence without loss of pay may not, however, exceed 30 days at one time. The Florida statute also provides that all employers—private and public—are prohibited from discharging, reprimanding, or in any other way penalizing any member of the Florida National Guard because of his or her absence resulting from active duty.

New York

In New York, the state's military law guarantees public employees their salary or other compensation for up to 30 working days.

California

The California law provides an unpaid leave of absence of (a) up to 17 calendar days a year for employees who are members of the Reserve Corps of the Armed Forces of the United States, of the National Guard, or of the Naval Militia and are engaged in military training; and (b) up to 15 calendar days for employees who are members of the State Military Reserve and are engaged in military training.

CHAPTER 9

JURY, WITNESS, AND VOTING DUTY

Jury Duty

Employer Requirements

Federal, state, and some local laws require that employers provide an employee with time off to serve as a juror in response to a court summons. The conditions for jury service in federal courts are controlled by the federal Jury Systems Improvement Act of 1978 (JSIA). Under the broad protections of the statute, an employer may not "discharge, threaten to discharge, intimidate, or coerce any employee" who receives a jury duty assignment. Employees must be guaranteed their job and seniority on returning to work, as well as any benefits that are normally provided under company policy to other workers who take leaves of absence.

Employers risk a violation of JSIA or of some state laws for committing any of the following actions: discharging or threatening workers with termination or with loss of benefits for taking jury duty leave; denying benefits during the period of leave, if company policy continues benefits for employees on other types of leave; requiring employees to postpone jury duty until sufficient vacation time has accrued to cover the length of jury service; or taking punitive action against employees upon their return to work from jury leave.

Employee Obligations

Employees should be informed that they must notify employers immediately upon receiving a summons for jury duty. Some states require employees to notify their employers on the first workday following receipt of a summons so that employers are best able to plan for an employee's absence.

Postponement of Jury Duty

Jury duty may be postponed when service constitutes a hardship for either the employee or the employer. Most states permit at least one postponement and an employer's request is likely to be granted during a busy season or when the employee's absence would leave the employer without an adequate workforce. The method of deferment varies from state to state, but detailed instructions are usually included on the court summons.

Payment of Salary during Duty

Federal law and most state laws do not require that an employer compensate workers during their service as jurors. Those states and local jurisdictions that *do* require the payment of salary during jury duty vary in their regulations.

For example, New York law requires employers with 10 or more employees to compensate for the first 3 days of duty at a rate of $40 per day. In Broward County, Florida, an employer cannot withhold wages for the first 5 days of jury duty, excluding the statutory jury fee earned by the employee.

In the absence of specific state or local requirements regarding the payment of wages during jury duty leave, employers may set their own compensation policies, provided that they are applied consistently and fairly to all.

Work Schedule during Duty

If an employee is excused from jury duty early on any day during the leave period, an employer may require the employee to report to work. Some state laws, however, prohibit this requirement if compliance would cause an undue burden on the employee, such as if extremely long travel distances are involved. Employers should also consider the performance implications when deciding whether to require night shift employees to work simultaneously with daytime jury duty.

Witness Duty

While there is no federal law requiring leave to appear as a witness, many states restrict employers from discharging an employee for taking leave to be a witness. Even in those states, the laws vary as to the conditions under which an employee is protected from termination for taking witness duty leave, as well as in the remedies and penalties for violations by employers.

For example, several states protect an employee from discharge for taking leave to be a witness in any civil case. Other states impose one or more of the following restrictions for an employee to be protected as a witness in a civil case: (a) the employee is required to be acting in response to a subpoena, (b) coverage is provided for public employees only, (c) reasonable notice must be given to the employer, (d) an employee who is a litigant or who appears by reason of his or her own misconduct is excluded from protection, or (e) the employee must be participating in a proceeding involving dependent children.

Employers in many states are also prevented from discharging employees who take leave to be witnesses in criminal proceedings. Several states apply one or more of the following types of restriction for a criminal case witness to be protected: (a) the employee must be the crime victim, (b) the employee may not be a litigant or be appearing by reason of his or her own misconduct, (c) the employee must be a public employee, (d) reasonable notice to the employer must be given, (e) the employee must be acting in response to a subpoena, or (f) the employee may not be the criminal defendant.

Employers who violate state provisions governing witness duty leave can be subject to fines or to misdemeanor imprisonment. Several states permit an employee to bring a civil action for lost wages, reinstatement, benefits, and reasonable attorney's fees.

Voting Duty

In the absence of any federal statute to guide employers on voting duty leave, more than 30 states have passed laws that require employers to grant employees time off to vote. Although the laws vary from state to state, such laws typically regulate the type of election to which the provisions apply, the amount of time that employees may take off from work to vote, and whether employers may deduct pay for lost time.

Most state laws require employers to give employees 2 or 3 consecutive hours off from work so that they may vote, provided that a period of time to vote is not available before the beginning of the regular workday or between the end of the regularly scheduled workday and the closing of the polls. Employers must consider the distance between where an employee lives and the workplace to determine how much time off is appropriate for voting purposes. To comply, employers may choose to allow employees to arrive late, depart early, or set aside a certain number of hours during the workday to permit sufficient time for voting.

CHAPTER 10

RELIGIOUS LEAVE

Employers are required to make provisions for religious observance by employees under Title VII of the Civil Rights Act. Most state discrimination statutes have the same requirement. This obligation, however, does not require employers to provide paid leave or to make accommodations that would cause the employer undue hardship. To meet this obligation, employers may designate a specific number of religious observance days for all employees, or may allow the use of paid personal or vacation days given to all employees for the purposes of accommodating religious needs. In some circumstances, even more is required. In addition to work-time conflicts with religious holidays, employees may seek prayer breaks mandated by religious beliefs or time off for religious mourning periods for deceased relatives.

Reasonable Accommodations under Title VII

Title VII's reasonable accommodation provision extends beyond beliefs or practices formally required by a person's religion. As long as an employee is sincerely motivated by religious beliefs, accommodation may be required. Therefore, a "religious" holiday requiring a leave period as an accommodation does not have to be one that is widely recognized, or even one that the employee has regularly observed in the past. When an employee requests leave for a religious holiday because of a sincere religious belief that work on the particular day is prohibited, the employer must, absent an undue hardship, accommodate the request even if the employee has admitted to not being devout or particularly observant. For example, if an employee sincerely held a religious belief that work on Sunday should be avoided—even though he occasionally worked from 11 P.M. to midnight on Sundays—the employer must try to find a reasonable accommodation. (In appropriate circumstances, an employer may consider refusing an employee's request for religious accommodation when the beliefs at issue appear to be more appropriately characterized as personal rather than religious beliefs, or when requests for accommodation appear to have been made in bad faith.)

Courts have held that an employer satisfies Title VII by attempting to find a co-worker who is willing to exchange shifts with an employee who needs time off as a religious accommodation, or by permitting the religious employee to find a co-worker who will volunteer to switch shifts. If, however, the employee's religion prohibits him or her from finding a replacement, the latter accommodation may not be sufficient.

Several federal appellate courts have required that, at a minimum, a reasonable accommodation must eliminate the conflict between employment requirements and religious practices. For example, if an employer refused to grant a Jewish employee's request for a day off on Yom Kippur, but offered another day off instead, this action would fail to provide a reasonable accommodation under Title VII because that proposed accommodation would not eliminate the conflict between the employees' religious beliefs and their employment duties. It is not necessarily the employee's burden to propose a workable accommodation to the employer. However, an employee requiring a period of leave as a religious accommodation has a duty to cooperate in the accommodation process.

It is the responsibility of the employee to notify the employer of impending specific conflicts between his or her religious needs and the scheduled work time, and for the notification to be reasonably in advance of the conflicts. Once an employer is on notice that an employee needs to leave work early on a weekday for religious activities, such as to attend a Wednesday night church service or to avoid secular work after sundown on a Friday, the employer must make an effort to accommodate the religious needs without adopting a wait-and-see posture on a week-by-week basis.

The EEOC's religious discrimination guidelines have suggested the following types of leave with which employers can reasonably accommodate an employee's religious conflict: flexible work breaks, staggered work hours, flexible arrival and departure times, floating or optional holidays, substitution of lunch breaks for an early departure, and replacement of time lost because of religious obligations.

If the timing of a religious leave of absence is not part of a bona fide religious belief, an employer does not have to accommodate for the leave. For example, if an employee requests a leave of absence during the busiest month at work for a 10-day pilgrimage and the timing of the trip was one of personal preference, denial of that request would not violate Title VII.

An employer does not have to grant a request for leave for a religious accommodation if to do so would create an undue hardship on the employer. Examples of undue hardship include (a) incurring additional labor costs to replace an employee, (b) causing conflict with a collective bargaining agreement, (c) requiring another employee to replace the religious employee, and (d) causing productivity losses. For example, if a Seventh Day Adventist sought shift exemptions from required training as a police recruit because his religion prohibited work from sundown on Friday through sundown on Saturday, the employer would not have to make this accommodation because the employee would have received training that was markedly different from that of other recruits. This difference would result in more than a de minimis impact on the health and safety concerns associated with police work.

Employers should be cautious about relying on the financial condition of their business as part of the undue hardship analysis, because courts have held that an employer's poor financial condition will not give rise to an exemption to the reasonable accommodation requirements. It is also recommended that employers should minimize the risk of liability and should attempt to accommodate an employee before claiming undue hardship. For example, an employer with a collective bargaining agreement should still consider providing a religious accommodation that does not conflict with the contract, such as a voluntary shift swap, if an employee is not sufficiently senior to avoid being scheduled for work on a day when he or she is unable to work for religious reasons.

PART TWO: LEAVE AS AN EMPLOYEE BENEFIT

CHAPTER 11

DISABILITY LEAVE

Short-Term Disability Leave

Several states—and even some local jurisdictions—have mandated that employees receive short-term disability benefits if they are ill or injured and are unable to work. States that mandate short-term disability benefits include California, Hawaii, New Jersey, New York, and Rhode Island. For example, a disabled employee in New York is entitled to a statutory payment of one-half of the employee's average weekly wage, with a maximum weekly benefit of $170 (for disabilities commencing on or after May 1, 1989), for a period of 26 weeks. Although Florida has not mandated short-term disability benefits, Miami–Dade County has enacted a short-term (4 month) disability ordinance.

When disability coverage is not required by law, an employer may voluntarily provide employees with short-term disability benefits. An employee handbook serves as a communication tool with which the employer can notify employees that short-term disability benefits are available. These benefits usually take the form of paid sick leave (discussed in chapter 13) or salary continuance (discussed next).

Long-Term Disability Leave

The employee handbook should contain a section that describes the duration, amount, and conditions of coverage.

Long-term disability benefits are not required by any state laws. When they choose to provide this coverage, a frequent issue that employers confront is when they may legally terminate an employee who is on long-term disability leave, an issue that is distinct from the duration of benefits paid to an employee while on long-term disability leave. To protect the employer, the policy should explain this distinction. Even though there may be cases when the amount of leave may have to be extended for an employee with an ADA disability, it is recommended that the policy provide for a leave of absence of up to a given maximum number of months. These "wooden" maximums provide the employer with a fixed standard against which the exceptions can be measured.

Employees who apply for long-term disability leave must be completely unable to work. The law is still unsettled as to whether or not an employee who claims to be completely disabled for the purpose of gaining coverage under a long-term disability policy can be simultaneously protected under the ADA—either that employee is not a qualified individual who can perform the essential functions of the job or the employer has a duty to reasonably accommodate the employee even though the employee has signed a benefits form declaring that he or she cannot work. Some courts hold that the ADA does not apply because an employee who purportedly cannot work at all is not qualified. Other courts have held that what an employee says when applying for long-term disability leave benefits is not binding on the issue of whether a reasonable accommodation is required.

Salary Continuation Policies

Either in addition to short-term disability benefits or instead of short-term disability benefits (where not state mandated), many employers provide salary continuation plans as part of their overall employee sick leave benefits. Salary continuation programs are similar to statutory short-term disability benefits in that they (a) provide employees with at least partial income continuance; (b) usually commence after a short waiting period (for example, 1 week); and (c) last for a longer period of time than do sick days (for example, up to 6 months).

CHAPTER 12

EMPLOYEE ASSISTANCE PROGRAMS

Many employers have established Employee Assistance Programs (EAPs) to assist employees with drug, alcohol, psychological, or related problems. EAP policies can provide for a wide range of treatment, including hospitalization and short-term counseling sessions. Therefore, an employee in an EAP is likely to require a leave of absence from work.

Despite the cost incurred, employers benefit from EAPs because the issues that are addressed through the program (such as marital, mental health, and substance abuse problems) can adversely affect an employee's work performance. Permitting an employee time off to receive help from an EAP alleviates absenteeism, misconduct, disruptive behavior, and work relationship problems. In addition to providing for a leave of absence, employers' EAP policies usually provide job security upon an employee's successful intervention and treatment.

An EAP leave policy should set out a mechanism for referral to the program. The first step for an employee to become eligible for EAP-related leave is through self-referrals, co-worker referrals, or manager referrals. Employers should train supervisors and managers to become familiar with the symptoms of chemical dependency and related problems so that they are equipped to identify problems and to facilitate appropriate intervention for employees who may require a leave of absence to participate in an EAP. A subsequent assessment by an EAP counselor can determine the method of treatment, which in turn determines the amount of a leave.

Some employers describe their EAP policies in their personnel manuals. These descriptions, especially any statements made regarding the confidentiality of an employee's treatment, must be carefully drafted to avoid a promise of absolute or strict confidentiality. Even where EAP information must be shared with those who need to know, all EAP-related information and/or communications should be handled with the utmost discretion, and employers should be aware that public disclosure of private facts concerning an employee, even if true, may subject the employer to tort claims for invasion of privacy. Therefore, unless there is a need to know, other employees should not be informed about the nature of an employee's absence caused by participation in EAP services.

Employers may be compelled to act in a manner consistent with their EAP policies. For example, an employer who gives employees information about the available crisis and substance abuse programs, who encourages employees to participate, and who promises job security cannot terminate an employee on the basis of his or her participation in an EAP alcohol abuse program.

CHAPTER 13

PAID LEAVES

Most, if not all, employers provide their employees with a package of benefits including several forms of time off from work. Some of this time off, however, is regulated by federal or state laws or both.

Vacation Leave

Anecdotally speaking, the most frequently read section of the employee handbook is the vacation pages. Therefore, it's not surprising that most employers provide employees with vacation time, which is usually in the form of paid leave. Employers may set a deadline for an employee's request for vacation time and may require advance approval of the request for time off.

A number of states have enacted wage payment statutes requiring employers who provide vacation benefits to pay accrued unused vacation to employees who terminate their employment. Consequently, in those states, an employer may not be able to have a policy stating that employees forfeit accrued vacation time upon termination. (For employers not in those states, it is recommended that the word "forfeit" be used in any policy that provides for the non-payment of accrued vacation for any reason, whether it be termination, resignation, or failure to provide adequate notice of resignation.) Thus, an employer should carefully describe how employees accrue vacation time.

For example, instead of stating that an employee accrues 10 vacation days annually, an employer might state that the employee accrues vacation time on a monthly basis, at a rate of $^{10}/_{12}$ of a vacation day per month. In fact, for the employee who is employed from January through December, this type of policy provides the same 10 annual vacation days. For the terminating employee, however, a monthly accrual policy allows the employer to pay that employee for vacation time on a prorated basis according to the number of months that the employee has actually worked.

Examples of states that have enacted these no-forfeiture laws include California, which requires that vacation time be paid to the employee as wages at the time the employment ends; Maryland, which defines wages as including a fringe benefit, although Maryland does not specifically define what constitutes a fringe benefit; and New York where (a) vacation time is considered wages that are required to be paid to a terminated employee not later than the regular payday for the pay period during which the termination occurred, and (b) employers are required to notify employees of their policies concerning "sick leave, vacation, personal leave, holidays, and hours."

In addition, even if a particular state has not enacted a statute regulating such payments, an employer should ascertain whether the courts, through case law, have required that employers pay accrued vacation time upon separation.

Sick Leave

Employers either may choose to or may be required to grant employees time off from work because of a brief sickness. As to the latter, chapter 2 on FMLA, contains a complete discussion for when an employee has a serious health condition that entitles him or her to sick leave.

Employers that allow the accumulation of sick leave may also choose to pay out unused sick leave upon separation. The Employee Retirement Income Security Act does not apply to accumulation payout programs because the payment is not a benefit payable in the event of sickness, but is rather an incentive to the employee to forgo use of sick leave.

Amounts paid to employees for the time they are absent from work on sick leave are deductible by the employer if such payments are ordinary and necessary business expenses. Sick pay paid by the employer is subject to mandatory income tax withholding. Sick leave payments received by an employee under personal health or accident insurance or under an employer's health or accident plan are also includable as income and are subject to federal income tax withholding.

Some states may require an employer to allow paid sick leave to be used for purposes other than an employee's own absence. For employers who are not in those states and who do not provide paid sick leave for the care of relatives, an employee who takes FMLA leave for the serious health condition of a child, spouse, or parent is not entitled to use paid sick leave as part of FMLA.

Comprehensive Leave

Comprehensive leave is a combination of sick leave and disability leave policies. There are basically two approaches for this leave. Under the first, employers give employees a set number of sick days per year and allow employees to bank unused leave up to a certain maximum amount. Employees are then required to use up their banked sick leave time before they may use short-term disability leave. Under the second approach, employers allot no set number of days per year for sick leave, and allow employees to take time off as needed for illness up to a set absenteeism amount. If the employee becomes short-term disabled, salary continuation would apply according to the length of service.

Personal Leave or Bereavement Leave

An employer is not legally required to grant personal leave. Many employers, however, grant leaves of absence for nonwork-related reasons, provided the employee's supervisor can spare the employee for the requested period of time. Personal leaves may be granted with or without pay, and employers have no obligation to hold a job for an employee unless they have explicitly agreed to do so.

Bereavement leave is an example of personal leave that may be permitted by an employer and is usually paid to full-time employees. Most employers grant short-term leave for a death in the family, and they often consider requests on a case-by-case basis regarding necessary travel and other arrangements. The amount of time permitted for bereavement leave is often determined by the degree of relationship of the employee to the family member. A day off is frequently permitted to allow employees to attend the funeral of a colleague from the same company.

Time Banks

Employers may provide time banks for unused vacation, personal, or sick leave. Instead of paying for unused leave time, employers allow leave to accumulate up to a certain maximum amount and be banked for the employee's use during the next relevant time period. Some employers permit employees to donate banked leave time to other employees for personal or health emergencies.

Holiday Leave

Official holidays declared by the federal or state governments are often mandatory with respect to employment in the public sector. While only a few states regulate holiday schedules for the private sector, the majority of employers have policies that permit the observance of certain popular holidays with paid time off from the workplace. Additionally, state and local laws may prohibit employers from conducting business on certain days of the calendar year.

For their holiday policies, employers should prepare and distribute to all employees a notice designating the specific observed holidays. Employees should be informed as far in advance as is practicable of any changes to the holiday schedule, including those relating to holidays that fall on weekends. Employers should also set clear guidelines for whether employees will receive holiday pay when the holiday coincides with other paid leave time such as jury duty or vacation.

Employers may require a minimum length of service for employees to be eligible for holiday pay, and may penalize employees by denying holiday pay if the employee takes unauthorized absences on the days preceding or following a holiday. Employers should specify what excuses, if any, are acceptable for absences taken directly before or after a holiday.

Sabbaticals

Sabbaticals are extended periods of personal leave that can be paid or unpaid. They are most commonly provided for managers or upper-level executives who want to join the political arena, gain additional education, or merely get relief from corporate burnout. Sabbaticals can also help employees to prepare for retirement. In some instances, sabbaticals are part of a formal company program, while in other instances, leaves are granted on a case-by-case basis. In deciding whether to grant sabbaticals, employers will generally take into account the employee's performance record and the reasons given for the requested time off. There is usually a substantial minimum service requirement.

Union-Related Leave Issues

Employer Obligations Regarding Leave to Conduct Union Business

In most cases, an employer may deny employees a leave of absence to conduct union business. If, however, there is a past practice to allow employees time off for union activities or if there is an established leave policy in a collective bargaining agreement, an employer must comply with the prior practices or provisions. Otherwise, an employer is obligated only to treat employees who are participating in union activities the same as employees who are engaged in non-union activities.

Prohibitions on Pay and Benefits during Union Leave

While in most cases an employer may use its discretion to grant time off to an employee for union-related activities, federal law may prohibit an employer from providing pay and benefits during the leave. Section 302(a) of the Labor-Management Relations Act (LMRA), as amended by the Taft-Hartley Act, provides that it is a criminal violation for any employer

> to pay, lend, or deliver, or agree to pay, lend, or deliver, any money or other thing of value (1) to any representative of any of his employees who are employed in an industry affecting commerce; or (2) to any labor organization, or to any officer or employee thereof, which represents, seeks to represent or would admit to membership, any of the employees of such employer who are employed in an industry affecting commerce....

Potential Liability for Providing Pay and Benefits during Union Leave

Any employer who violates Section 302(a) of the LMRA can be punished with fines of up to $15,000 or imprisonment for up to 5 years or both. Intended to prevent the bribery of union officials, the statute's broad application applies not only to salaries, but also to benefits and employee leave. Employers are prohibited from providing a "thing of value" to any employee who is representing other employees or acting in the capacity of a union official.

An employer is, however, allowed to provide a "thing of value" and to pay employees on union leave if there is a "no-docking" policy in effect in the workplace for full-time employees who spend brief periods of time on union business. An employer may also provide pension credit and other benefits during an employee's leave to be a full-time union official if such payment is pursuant to a collective bargaining agreement provision that was in effect before the leave began, or is pursuant to a nondiscretionary leave policy that employees had notice of.

The Establishment of Leave Benefits under Collective Bargaining Agreements

An employer is required to collectively bargain with a union under the National Labor Relations Act (NLRA) "with respect to wages, hours, and other terms and conditions of employment." Leave provisions are considered mandatory subjects of bargaining because they involve the terms and conditions of employment.

The Overlay of the ADA and FMLA on the Collective Bargaining Process

An employer has a duty to bargain with a union regarding the ADA accommodations that constitute changes in terms and conditions of employment, such as (a) restructuring an existing job, (b) granting a shift change or transfer, (c) reassigning an employee to a vacant position, (d) implementing a part-time or modified work schedule, (e) granting a leave of absence, or (f) placing a returning disabled employee in a position for which he or she lacks seniority under the collective bargaining agreement. An employer may not unilaterally implement a reasonable accommodation for a disabled employee who returns to work if the accommodation is a material, substantial, or significant change in working conditions. If an accommodation does not materially alter the collective working conditions of other employees, the employer may implement it without bargaining with the union. If a proposed accommodation conflicts with the collective bargaining agreement, such as when the disabled employee needs a leave that is contractually "guaranteed" to a more senior employee, the employer should notify and bargain with the union provided that the employee has consented to the employer's disclosing the disability to the union. An employer who bypasses the union to determine the appropriate accommodation by conferring with an employee may be engaged in "direct dealing" with the employee in violation of the NLRA.

Employers are also required to bargain with the union over several specific FMLA leave issues. Bargaining is mandated to determine (a) which method to use to measure the 12-month period, (b) whether employees must use paid time off during the leave, (c) whether the employer will require a 30-day advance notice, (d) whether benefits provided by the employer will continue during the leave, and (e) whether FMLA contract benefits will extend beyond the FMLA requirements to sites with fewer than 50 employees or to employees with less than 1,250 hours. Employers should also be aware of the impact that any seniority provisions in a collective bargaining agreement will have on the placement of employees returning from FMLA leave.

Meals and Rest Periods

Unless it is specifically designated as compensated working time by an employment contract, an employer is not required to compensate an employee for a bona fide meal period. According to Department of Labor regulations, a "bona fide" meal period exists only when an employee is excused from regular work responsibilities for 30 minutes or more to eat a meal. The employer must compensate the employee if he or she is required to perform any inactive duties while eating, or if the employee is required to remain "on call" during the break. For example, employees who are required to eat at their desks or machines are engaged in inactive work and must be compensated for the time. If, however, an employee is required to remain on the premises of the employer during a bona fide meal period, it is noncompensable time.

Full-time employees usually receive one unpaid lunch break during each scheduled workday. Breaks may range from one-half hour to a full hour, depending on industry custom. In some states, the amount of meal time for particular classes of workers, including factory workers and minors, is determined by statute. Employees who work overtime in a single workday are usually permitted a second meal break for dinner.

Employers should treat rest periods of 20 minutes or less as compensable time. Therefore, short breaks for snacks or coffee should not be deducted from an employee's daily hours.

PART THREE: IMPLEMENTING LEAVE PROCEDURES

CHAPTER 14

IMPLEMENTATION PROCEDURES

Expressing Leave Policy Components

Employee Handbooks

The employee handbook is a good place to describe an employer's leave policies (such as vacation, holiday, personal time, and sick leave). A handbook can advise the workforce of important policies and procedures; can ensure consistent treatment of all employees regarding leave issues; and can memorialize the employer's commitment to comply with all federal, state, and local laws pertaining to leave. The provisions should be clear, consistent, and regularly updated. All employees should be required to sign an Acknowledgment of Receipt of Policy Form so that employers can rebut later claims by employees that they were unaware of specific leave provisions.

Employers should be aware that in preparing their handbook's leave policies they are drafting a quasi-legal document that must be thoughtfully and carefully assembled. Courts in many states have found that employee handbooks, under certain circumstances, create express or implied contracts, and these courts have awarded substantial verdicts against employers for breach of their handbook provisions. In drafting the provisions, employers should avoid using terms that could be interpreted to create binding obligations, such as "promise" or "contract." To avoid liability, employers should consider carefully drafting a disclaimer in accordance with state law so they advise employees that the policies and procedures are not intended to create a contract of employment, and so they explicitly reserve the right to modify or discontinue the leave policies at any time.

Other Communication Tools

Although such tools are not part of the employee handbook, federal and state laws mandate that employers display posters within each work facility to inform employees about certain regulations and benefits. Those posters must be publicly displayed in a prominent location. One of the federal posters that an employer is required to post in the workplace is a discussion of the provisions of the FMLA, including its leave provisions. Employers could also communicate leave policies through newsletters or bulletin boards placed in common areas.

Dissemination of Leave Policies

Employers should ensure that human resources representatives and supervisors are well informed about leave policies. Informational meetings between human resources personnel and employees are an effective way to explain and answer questions about the leave policies contained in an employee handbook. To promote consistency when applying leave policies, employers should designate a centralized administrator to answer all leave-related inquiries and to ensure that employees are well informed regarding any updates to leave policies.

CHAPTER 15

ADDRESSING IMPLEMENTATION POLICY OPTIONS

Developing Procedures that an Employee Must Follow When Requesting Leave

A clearly drafted section on procedures should be included in an employee handbook to eliminate employees' common misconception that they are legally entitled to leave time without having to follow established formalities. Employers should include provisions for how employees should request leave time, procedures to follow upon return, specific instructions on requesting extensions, and the consequences for failing to comply with the guidelines.

Oral and Written Requests for Leave

In policy statements, employers should clearly designate how different leave periods will be authorized. Statements should include whether a form must be filled out or whether an informal oral request is sufficient, which specific individual the employee should notify regarding the request, and what detailed information must be included with the request. In addition, the policy should give employees a timeline for how far in advance they should submit requests for leave.

Medical Benefit Continuation during Leave

Most employers permit medical benefits to continue during short- and long-term leaves of absence from work. Terminating medical benefits during a leave period could be harmful to the health of an individual who is on leave for medical reasons or who is disabled and could result in significant damage to employee morale and recruitment potential.

Specific federal legislation regulates the continuation of medical benefits during leave. For example, the FMLA, discussed previously, requires employers to maintain medical and health benefits during a family- or medical leave-related absence under the same conditions as if the employee had continued to work.

Seniority Accrual during Leave

The majority of employers permit seniority to accrue during a leave of absence. Others choose to lock in an employee's status until he or she returns to work or to set time limits on accrual for particular types of leave. However, when an employee is legally guaranteed seniority status, such as for military leave or pursuant to a union contract, employers must comply with their legal obligations.

Vacation and Benefit Credits

Either most employers do not permit vacation credits to accrue while an employee is out on leave or they allow vacation credits to accrue only up to a certain time limit. An employer should issue a policy statement that addresses vacation credits and that specifies whether benefits coverage during leave will include continued payments for life insurance, medical and disability insurance, pension or profit sharing plans, or savings. Employers that choose not to continue coverage during an absence may allow employees to pay the premiums at group rates on their own until they return from leave.

Addressing Leave Policy Abuse

The employee handbook should contain provisions addressing disciplinary action for failure to comply with leave policy provisions, with language that allows for a wide range of circumstances to be addressed. Disregard of the required procedures regarding authorization of leave or misrepresentation of the nature of leave are examples of conduct that would warrant disciplinary action up to and including dismissal. Employers should make sure that any disciplinary action taken against an employee for a violation of leave policies conforms with the provisions in the handbook.

In addition, to prevent policy abuse, employers may require periodic medical updates and verification from employees who are out on leave.

Reemployment Entitlements

An employer's approval of a leave of absence is an implied promise that the employee will be reemployed in his or her position upon return. Under some circumstances, however, such as when a job position has been eliminated entirely, an employer will have to assign the returning employee to a substitute position. The employee handbook should designate when a position substitution by the employer can be expected. When such a situation occurs, an employer should endeavor to provide a substitute position that is comparable in seniority and salary, and should be aware of any collective bargaining agreement provisions regarding reemployment, including those provisions that may impact on the rights of any union worker who is replaced by an employee returning from leave.

Leave Cancellation

Employers should develop specific policies for the conditions under which leave may be canceled, and should apply such policies to all employees in a consistent, nondiscriminatory fashion. The conditions should be contained within the employee handbook or otherwise effectively communicated to employees. Employer policies may provide that leave be canceled if the business would reasonably be adversely affected by an absence, such as when leave of several employees at the same time would result in severe understaffing in a particular department, or when client or customer needs must be satisfied. Issues to be addressed in a cancellation policy include rescheduling, vacation carryover, and reimbursement, if any, for nonrefundable deposits.

The Effect of Layoffs on Leave

In making decisions about employee terminations, employers should take care not to discriminate against employees merely because they are out on leave. If layoffs occur throughout the company, an employer should, at the same time, notify any employee out on leave that he or she will be terminated. Termination of employees who are absent for family, medical, jury duty, military duty, or union business leave may violate their right to reinstatement.

Setting Time Limits on Leave

While the duration of some leave is statutorily mandated, employers will routinely set minimum or maximum time limits for other types of absences. To determine the amount of time off that will be permitted, employers should factor in the length of time an employee has been with the company, the reasons for the leave, and the time the leave will occur. The time limits for each type of leave should be clearly stated in the employee handbook. The handbook provisions should also explain how extensions should be requested and under what circumstances, if any, they may be approved.

APPENDIX A

SAMPLE POLICY STATEMENTS AND HANDBOOK PROVISIONS

Family and Medical Leave Act Policy

[NOTE TO EMPLOYER: This policy is intended to comply with the Federal Family and Medical Leave Act of 1993 and the regulations issued by the U.S. Department of Labor pursuant to the Act. As of July 1995, it may be used in New York and other jurisdictions that do not have a state or local statute governing family or medical leave.]

The Family and Medical Leave Act (FMLA) provides eligible employees with up to 12 workweeks of unpaid leave for certain family and medical reasons during a 12-month period. During this leave, an eligible employee is entitled to continued group health plan coverage as if the employee had continued to work. At the conclusion of the leave, subject to some exceptions, an employee generally has a right to return to the same or to an equivalent position.

Eligibility

To be eligible for FMLA leave, an employee must have been employed by **[Employer]**:

(i) for at least 12 months (which need not be consecutive);

(ii) for at least 1250 hours during the 12-month period immediately preceding the commencement of the leave; <u>and</u>

(iii) at a worksite (a) with 50 or more employees; or (b) where 50 or more employees are located within 75 miles of the worksite.

Reasons for FMLA Leave

FMLA leave may be taken for any one, or for a combination of, the following reasons:

- the birth of the employee's child or to care for the newborn child;
- the placement of a child with the employee for adoption or foster care or to care for the newly placed child;
- to care for the employee's spouse, child or parent (but not in-law) with a serious health condition; and/or
- the employee's own serious health condition that makes the employee unable to perform one or more of the essential functions of his or her job.

A "serious health condition" is an injury, illness, impairment, or physical or mental condition that involves inpatient care or continuing treatment by a health care provider.

[NOTE TO EMPLOYER: A more detailed definition of "serious health condition" can be found in the Department of Labor's Certification of Health Care Provider Form (Form WH-380-December 1994).]

How Much and When FMLA Leave May Be Taken

The 12-Month Period

An eligible employee is entitled to up to 12 workweeks of unpaid leave during a 12-month period for any FMLA qualifying reason(s). The 12-month period is **[Insert one of the alternatives below]**.

> **[NOTE TO EMPLOYER: Before issuing this policy, the Employer should select one of the following methods for calculating the 12-month period. Alternatively, the Employer may choose to designate any other fixed 12-month period in lieu of the alternatives listed below. The method chosen should be uniformly applied and may not be changed without notice. Note that under each of the alternatives, with the exception of the "rolling backward 12-month period," it is possible for an employee to take all or part of his/her FMLA leave at the**

conclusion of one year and to take an additional 12 weeks at the beginning of the following year.

- the calendar year.
- [Employer's] fiscal year.
- the 12 months beginning on the employee's anniversary date of employment.
- the 12-month period measured forward from the date an employee's first FMLA leave begins. Subsequent 12-month periods begin the first time FMLA leave is taken after the completion of any previous 12-month period.
- a rolling 12-month period measured backward from the date an employee uses any FMLA leave.]

Limitations on FMLA Leave

Leave to care for a newborn or for a newly placed child must conclude within 12 months after the birth or placement of the child.

When both spouses are employed by **[Employer]**, they are together entitled to a combined total of 12 workweeks of FMLA leave within the designated 12 month period for the birth, adoption or foster care placement of a child with the employees, for aftercare of the newborn or newly placed child, and to care for a parent (but not in-law) with a serious health condition. Each spouse may be entitled to additional FMLA leave for other FMLA qualifying reasons (i.e., the difference between the leave taken individually for any of the above reasons and 12 workweeks, but not more than a total of 12 workweeks per person).

For example, if each spouse took 6 weeks of leave to care for a newborn child, each could later use an additional 6 weeks due to his/her own serious health condition or to care for a child with a serious health condition.

Intermittent or Reduced Work Schedule Leave

Intermittent leave is leave taken in separate blocks of time. A reduced work schedule leave is a leave schedule that reduces an employee's usual number of hours per workweek or hours per workday.

Leave to care for a newborn or for a newly placed child **[Insert one of the alternatives below]**.

[NOTE TO EMPLOYER: Before issuing this policy, the Employer should select one of the following:

- must be taken all at once and may not be taken intermittently or on a reduced work schedule.

- may not be taken intermittently or on a reduced work schedule unless [Employer] agrees with respect to an individual leave request.]

Leave because of an employee's own serious health condition, or to care for an employee's spouse, child or parent with a serious health condition, may be taken all at once or, where medically necessary, intermittently or on a reduced work schedule.

If an employee takes leave intermittently or on a reduced work schedule basis, the employee must, when requested, attempt to schedule the leave so as not to unduly disrupt the [Employer's] operations. When an employee takes intermittent or reduced work schedule leave for foreseeable planned medical treatment, [Employer] may temporarily transfer the employee to an alternative position with equivalent pay and benefits for which the employee is qualified and which better accommodates recurring periods of leave.

Requests for FMLA Leave

An employee should request FMLA leave by completing the Employer's Request for Leave form and submitting it to [Insert name of employer contact].

When leave is foreseeable for childbirth, placement of a child or planned medical treatment for the employee's or family member's serious health condition, the employee must provide [Employer] with at least 30 days advance notice, or such shorter notice as is practicable (i.e., within 1 or 2 business days of learning of the need for the leave). When the timing of the leave is not foreseeable, the employee must provide [Employer] with notice of the need for leave as soon as practicable (i.e., within 1 or 2 business days of learning of the need for the leave).

Required Documentation

When leave is taken to care for a family member, [Employer] may require the employee to provide documentation or statement of family relationship (e.g., birth certificate or court document).

Appendix A

An employee may be required to submit medical certification from a health care provider to support a request for FMLA leave for the employee's or a family member's serious health condition. Medical certification forms are available from **[Insert name of employer contact]**.

If **[Employer]** has reason to doubt the employee's initial certification, **[Employer]** may: (i) with the employee's permission, have a designated health care provider contact the employee's health care provider in an effort to clarify or authenticate the initial certification; and/or (ii) require the employee to obtain a second opinion by an independent **[Employer]**-designated provider at **[Employer's]** expense. If the initial and second certifications differ, **[Employer]** may, at its expense, require the employee to obtain a third, final, and binding certification from a jointly selected health care provider.

During FMLA leave, **[Employer]** may request that the employee provide recertification of a serious health condition at intervals in accordance with the FMLA. In addition, during FMLA leave, the employee must provide **[Employer]** with periodic reports regarding the employee's status and intent to return to work. If the employee's anticipated return to work date changes and it becomes necessary for the employee to take more or less leave than originally anticipated, the employee must provide **[Employer]** with reasonable notice (i.e., within 2 business days) of the employee's changed circumstances and new return to work date. If the employee gives **[Employer]** notice of the employee's intent not to return to work, the employee will be considered to have voluntarily resigned.

Before the employee returns to work from FMLA leave for the employee's own serious health condition, the employee may be required to submit a fitness for duty certification from the employee's health care provider, with respect to the condition for which the leave was taken, stating that the employee is able to resume work.

FMLA leave or return to work may be delayed or denied if the appropriate documentation is not provided in a timely manner. Also, a failure to provide requested documentation of the reason for an absence from work may lead to termination of employment.

Use of Paid and Unpaid Leave

FMLA provides eligible employees with up to 12 workweeks of unpaid leave. If an employee has accrued paid leave (e.g., vacation, sick leave, personal leave), however, the employee **[Insert one of the following alternatives: *must*** or *may*] use any qualifying paid leave first. "Qualifying paid leave" is leave that would otherwise be available to the employee for the purpose for which the FMLA leave is taken. The remainder of the 12 workweeks of leave, if any, will be unpaid FMLA leave. Any paid leave used for an FMLA qualifying reason will be charged against an employee's entitlement to FMLA leave. This includes leave for disability or workers' compensation injury/illness, provided that the leave meets FMLA requirements. The substitution of paid leave for unpaid leave does not extend the 12 workweek leave period.

> **[NOTE TO EMPLOYER: The FMLA gives the employer the right to require that the employee use qualifying paid leave prior to taking unpaid FMLA leave. In the alternative, the employee may elect to use qualifying paid leave.**
>
> **The Department of Labor takes the position that an employee's receipt of workers' compensation or disability payments precludes the employee from electing, and prohibits the employer from requiring, substitution of accrued paid leave for any part of the absence covered by such payments.]**

Designation of Leave

[Employer] will notify the employee that leave has been designated as FMLA leave. [Employer] may provisionally designate the employee's leave as FMLA leave if [Employer] has not received medical certification or has not otherwise been able to confirm that the employee's leave qualifies as FMLA leave. If the employee has not notified [Employer] of the reason for the leave, and the employee desires that leave be counted as FMLA leave, the employee must notify [Insert name of employer contact] within 2 business days of the employee's return to work that the leave was for an FMLA reason.

> **[NOTE TO EMPLOYER: It is the Employer's responsibility to designate leave, paid or unpaid, as FMLA qualifying and to give the employee notice of the designation.**
>
> **The Department of Labor takes the position that, absent extenuating circumstances, the Employer must give the employee notice of the designation within 2 business days after the Employer has acquired knowledge that leave is being taken for an FMLA qualifying reason. The notice may be written or oral but, if oral, must be confirmed in writing no later than the next payday that occurs one week or more after the oral notice.**

It is important to designate leave (whether paid or unpaid) as FMLA leave in a timely manner. Otherwise, for example, an employee who takes several weeks of paid sick leave that is not designated as FMLA leave may then be entitled to an additional 12 weeks of leave under the FMLA.]

Maintenance of Health Benefits

During FMLA leave an employee is entitled to continued group health plan coverage under the same conditions as if the employee had continued to work.

[NOTE TO EMPLOYERS: The second and third paragraphs of this section are not applicable to Employers with non-contributory group health plans.

With respect to the second paragraph, prepayment of premiums, whether pursuant to a cafeteria plan or otherwise, is permitted only if the employee agrees.

With respect to the third paragraph, an employee's health insurance coverage may be discontinued only after 15 days notice by the Employer. Note, however, that if coverage is discontinued and the employee returns from FMLA leave, the employee may not be required to meet any qualification requirements imposed by the group health plan (e.g., waiting period or medical examination).]

To the extent that an employee's FMLA leave is paid, the employee's portion of health insurance premiums will be deducted from the employee's salary. For the portion of FMLA leave that is unpaid, the employee's portion of health insurance premiums may be **[Insert one of the alternatives below]**.

[NOTE TO EMPLOYER: Before issuing this policy, the Employer should select one of the following methods for payment of the employee's portion of health insurance premiums.

- paid at the same time as if made by payroll deduction.
- paid on the same schedule as payments under COBRA.
- prepaid pursuant to a cafeteria plan.

- paid in accordance with the employer's rules for leave without pay.

- paid pursuant to a system voluntarily agreed to by [Employer] and the employee.]

If the employee's payment of health insurance premiums is more than 30 days late, [Employer] may discontinue health insurance coverage upon notice to the employee.

Return from FMLA Leave

Upon return from FMLA leave, [Employer] will place the employee in the same position the employee held before the leave or an equivalent position with equivalent pay, benefits, and other employment terms.

Limitations on Reinstatement

An employee is entitled to reinstatement only if he/she would have continued to be employed had FMLA leave not been taken. Thus, an employee is not entitled to reinstatement if, because of a layoff, reduction in force, or other reason, the employee would not be employed at the time job restoration is sought.

[Employer] reserves the right to deny reinstatement to salaried, eligible employees who are among the highest paid 10 percent of [Employer's] employees employed within 75 miles of the worksite ("key employees") if such denial is necessary to prevent substantial and grievous economic injury to [Employer's] operations.

Failure to Return to Work Following FMLA Leave

If the employee does not return to work following the conclusion of FMLA leave, the employee will be considered to have voluntarily resigned. [Employer] may recover health insurance premiums that [Employer] paid on behalf of the employee during any unpaid FMLA leave except that [Employer's] share of such premiums may not be recovered if the employee fails to return to work because of the employee's or a family member's serious health condition or because of other circumstances beyond the employee's control. In such cases, [Employer] may require the employee to provide medical certification of the employee's or the family member's serious health condition.

Appendix A

Additional Information

For further information or clarification about FMLA leave, please contact **[Insert name of employer contact]**.

Sample Family and Medical Leave Request Form

Background Information

Employee's Name _____ ID# _____

Full Time _____ Part Time _____ Employment Date __/__/__

Position _____ Department _____

Home Address _____

Home Telephone Number (___) _____

[If you will be unreachable at your home address and telephone number during the requested leave, please provide an address and phone number where you may be contacted.]

Address _____

Telephone Number (___) _____

If married, does your spouse work for **[Employer]**? ___ Yes ___ No

Request for Leave

I am requesting a leave (check all applicable blanks):

___ for the birth of my child

___ to care for my newborn child within 12 months of the birth

___ to adopt a child

___ to care for my newly adopted child within 12 months of the adoption

___ for the foster care placement of a child with me

___ to care for my newly placed foster child within 12 months of the placement

___ to care for my child with a serious health condition

___ to care for my parent with a serious health condition

Appendix A

___ to care for my spouse with a serious health condition

___ due to my own serious health condition

I would like leave to begin on ___/___/___.

I expect to return from leave on ___/___/___.

If intermittent leave (i.e., leave taken in separate blocks of time) or reduced work schedule FMLA leave (i.e., a leave schedule that reduces an employee's usual number of hours per workweek or hours per workday) is requested, please complete the following section. Note that leave to care for a newborn or newly placed child **[Insert one of the alternatives below]**.

> **[NOTE TO EMPLOYER: Before issuing this form, the Employer should select one of the following. Employer's selection should conform with selection made in the "Intermittent or Reduced Work Schedule Leave" section of the Sample FMLA Policy.**
>
> - **must be taken all at once and may not be taken intermittently or on a reduced work schedule.**
>
> - **may not be taken intermittently or on a reduced work schedule unless [Employer] agrees with respect to an individual leave request.]**

Please complete the following:

Day	Current Work Schedule	Proposed Work Schedule
Monday	___a.m./p.m. to ___a.m./p.m.	___a.m./p.m. to ___a.m./p.m.
Tuesday	___a.m./p.m. to ___a.m./p.m.	___a.m./p.m. to ___a.m./p.m.
Wednesday	___a.m./p.m. to ___a.m./p.m.	___a.m./p.m. to ___a.m./p.m.
Thursday	___a.m./p.m. to ___a.m./p.m.	___a.m./p.m. to ___a.m./p.m.
Friday	___a.m./p.m. to ___a.m./p.m.	___a.m./p.m. to ___a.m./p.m.
Saturday	___a.m./p.m. to ___a.m./p.m.	___a.m./p.m. to ___a.m./p.m.
Sunday	___a.m./p.m. to ___a.m./p.m.	___a.m./p.m. to ___a.m./p.m.

Other Schedule: _____

I would like to begin the intermittent or reduced work schedule leave on ___/___/___.

I expect to return from intermittent or reduced work schedule leave on ___/___/___.

> [NOTE TO EMPLOYER: The following section should be included in this form if you allow your employees to elect (rather than require them) to substitute qualifying paid leave for unpaid FMLA leave.]
>
> **Indicate the amount of qualifying accrued paid leave that you would like to use for FMLA leave. "Qualifying accrued paid leave" is leave that would otherwise be available to you for the purpose for which FMLA leave is taken. Note that any paid leave used during a leave that is covered by the FMLA will be counted against your entitlement to FMLA leave.**

Indicate below the dates that qualifying accrued paid time will be used; any remaining FMLA leave will be unpaid:

Vacation:	___/___/___	to	___/___/___
Sick:	___/___/___	to	___/___/___
Personal Leave:	___/___/___	to	___/___/___
Unpaid:	___/___/___	to	___/___/___

_____   Date ___/___/___
Employee's Signature

_____   Date ___/___/___
Supervisor's Signature

APPENDIX B

Sample Employer Response to Employee Request for Family or Medical Leave

TO: _____
   (*Employee's Name*)

FROM: _____
   (*Name of appropriate employer representative*)

SUBJECT: Request for Family/Medical Leave

DATE: ___/___/___

On _____, you notified us of your need to take family/medical leave due to:

- ☐ the birth of a child, or the placement of a child with you for adoption or foster care and/or to care for a newborn or newly placed child; or

- ☐ a serious health condition that makes you unable to perform the essential functions of your job; or

- ☐ a serious health condition affecting your ☐ spouse, ☐ child, ☐ parent, for which you are needed to provide care.

You notified us that you need this leave beginning on _____ and that you expect leave to continue until on or about _____.

Except as explained below, you have a right under the FMLA for up to 12 weeks of unpaid leave in a 12-month period for the reasons listed above. Also, your health benefits must be maintained during any period of unpaid leave under the same conditions as if you continued to work and, subject to some exceptions, you have a right to be reinstated to the same or an equivalent job with the same pay, benefits, and terms and conditions of employment on your return from leave. If you do not return to work following FMLA leave for a reason other than: (1) the continuation, recurrence, or onset of a serious health condition which would entitle you to FMLA leave; or (2) other circumstances beyond your control, you may be required to reimburse us for our share of health insurance premiums paid on your behalf during your FMLA leave.

This is to inform you that: **[NOTE TO EMPLOYER: check appropriate boxes; explain where indicated]**

1. You are ☐ *eligible*
   ☐ *not eligible*
   for leave under the FMLA.

2. The requested leave ☐ *will* ☐ *provisionally will, subject to submission or confirmation of required documentation,* ☐ *will not* be counted against your annual FMLA leave entitlement.

3. You ☐ *will* ☐ *will not* be required to furnish medical certification of a serious health condition. If required, you must furnish certification by _____ (*insert date*) (15 days after you are notified of this requirement) or we may delay the commencement of your leave until the certification is submitted.

4. You may elect to substitute accrued paid leave for unpaid FMLA leave. We ☐ *will* ☐ *will not* require that you substitute accrued paid leave for unpaid FMLA leave.

   [NOTE TO EMPLOYER: Employer selection in the foregoing sentence should conform with the selection made in the "Use of Paid and Unpaid Leave" section of the Sample FMLA Policy.]

If paid leave will be used, the following conditions will apply:

Appendix B

[NOTE TO EMPLOYER: Sub-paragraphs (a) and (b) of paragraph 5 are not applicable to Employers with non-contributory group health plans. The arrangements for payment in sub-paragraph (a) should conform with the selection made in the "Maintenance of Health Benefits" section of the Sample FMLA Policy.]

5. a. If you normally pay a portion of the premiums for your health insurance, these payments will continue during the period of FMLA leave. Arrangements for payment have been discussed with you and it is agreed that you will make premium payments as follows:

   b. You have a minimum 30 day [NOTE TO EMPLOYER: indicate longer period, if applicable] grace period in which to make premium payments. If timely payment is not made, your group health insurance may be canceled, provided we notify you in writing at least 15 days before the date that your health coverage will lapse or, at our option, we may pay your share of the premiums during FMLA leave, and recover these payments from you upon the conclusion of your leave.

   [NOTE TO EMPLOYER: If Employer has other contributory benefit plans (e.g., life or disability insurance), Employer may want to address the issue of premium payments during unpaid FMLA leave by inserting sub-paragraph (c). The Department of Labor takes the position that the Employer is required to follow its policy or practice for other unpaid leaves or, if there is no established policy, to agree upon arrangements with the employee. The employee may elect to continue these benefits. Alternatively, the Employer may elect to maintain such benefits (even if the employee does not) in light of the Employer's obligation to resume the employee's benefits at the same level and without qualification requirements upon the employee's return from leave. At the conclusion of leave, the Employer may recover the costs incurred for paying the employee's share of any premiums (whether or not the employee returns to work).]

c. If you normally pay a portion of premiums for other benefits (e.g., life or disability insurance, etc.), you may continue these benefits by making the required premium payments during the period of FMLA leave. Arrangements for payments have been discussed with you and it is agreed that you will make premium payments as follows:

We may, at our option, pay your share of premiums for other benefits while you are on FMLA leave and recover these payments from you at the conclusion of your leave.

6. You ☐ *will* ☐ *will not* be required to present a fitness-for-duty certificate prior to being restored to employment. If such certification is required but not received, your return to work may be delayed until certification is provided.

7. a. You ☐ *are* ☐ *are not* a "key employee." **[NOTE TO EMPLOYER: The definition of key employee is contained in the "Return From FMLA Leave-Limitations on Reinstatement" section of the Sample FMLA Policy and is described in §825.218 of the FMLA regulations.]** If you are a "key employee," restoration to employment may be denied following FMLA leave on the grounds that such restoration will cause substantial and grievous economic injury to your employer.

b. We ☐ *have* ☐ *have not* determined that restoring you to employment at the conclusion of FMLA leave will cause substantial and grievous economic harm to us. (*Explain (a) and/or (b) below.*)

Appendix B

8. While on leave, you ☐ *will* ☐ *will not* be required to furnish us with periodic reports every _____. **[NOTE TO EMPLOYER: indicate interval of periodic reports, as appropriate for the particular leave situation; see §825.309 of the FMLA regulations.]** of your status and intent to return to work. If the circumstances of your leave change and you are able to return to work earlier than the date indicated on the reverse side of this form, you ☐ *will* ☐ *will not* be required to notify us at least two work days prior to the date you intend to report for work.

9. You ☐ *will* ☐ *will not* be required to furnish recertification relating to a serious health condition. **[NOTE TO EMPLOYER: Explain below, if necessary, including the interval between certifications as prescribed in §825.308 of the FMLA regulations.]**

APPENDIX C

CERTIFICATION OF HEALTH CARE PROVIDER

Appendix B to Part 825—Certification of Health Care Provider (Optional Form WH-380)

Certification of Health
Care Provider
(Family and Medical Leave Act of 1993)

U.S. Department of Labor
Employment Standards Administration
Wage and Hour Division

1. Employee's Name

2. Patient's Name (if different from employee)

3. The attached sheet describes what is meant by a **"serious health condition"** under the Family and Medical Leave Act. Does the patient's condition[1] qualify under any of the categories described? If so, please check the applicable category.

   (1) _____ (2) _____ (3) _____ (4) _____ (5) _____ (6) _____ , or None of the above _____

4. Describe the **medical facts** which support your certification, including a brief statement as to how the medical facts meet the criteria of one of these categories:

5. a. State the approximate date the condition commenced, and the probable duration of the condition (and also the probable duration of the patient's present **Incapacity**[2] if different):

   b. Will It be necessary for the employee to take work only **Intermittently or to work on a less than full schedule** as a result of the condition (including for treatment described in Item 6 below)? _____

Appendix C

If yes, give the probable duration:

    c. If the condition is a **chronic condition** (condition #4) or **pregnancy**, state whether the patient is presently incapacitated [2] and the likely duration and frequency of **episodes of incapacity**[2]:

6. a. If additional **treatments** will be required for the condition, provide an estimate of the probable number of such treatments:

If the patient will be absent from work or other daily activities because of **treatment** on an **Intermittent** or **part-time** basis, also provide an estimate of the probable number and interval between such treatments, actual or estimated dates of treatment if known, and period required for recovery if any:

---

[1] Here and elsewhere on this form, the information sought relates **only** to the condition for which the employee is taking FMLA leave.

[2] **"Incapacity,"** for purposes of FMLA, is defined to mean inability to work, attend school or perform other regular daily activities due to the serious health condition, treatment therefor, or recovery therefrom.

Form WH-380
March 1995

b. If any of these treatments will be provided by **another provider of health services** (e.g., physical therapist), please state the nature of the treatments:

c. **If a regimen of continuing treatment** by the patient is required under your supervision, provide a general description of such regimen (e.g., prescription drugs, physical therapy requiring special equipment):

7. a. If medical leave is required for the employee's **absence from work** because of the **employee's own condition** (including absences due to pregnancy or a chronic condition), is the employee **unable to perform work** of any kind? _____

b. If able to perform some work, is the employee **unable to perform any one or more of the essential functions of the employee's job** (the employee or the employer should supply you with information about the essential job functions)? _____ If yes, please list the essential functions the employee is unable to perform:

c. If neither a. nor b. applies, is it necessary for the employee to be **absent from work for treatment?** _____

8. a. If leave is required to **care for a family member** of the employee with a serious health condition, **does the patient require assistance** for basic medical or personal needs or safety, or for transportation? _____

b. If no, would the employee's presence to provide **psychological comfort** be beneficial to the patient or assist in the patient's recovery? _____

Appendix C

c. If the patient will need care only **intermittently** or on a part-time basis, please indicate the probable **duration** of this need:

_____ _____
(Signature of Health Care Provider) (Type of Practice)

_____ _____
(Address) (Telephone Number)

To be completed by the employee needing family leave to care for a family member:

State the care you will provide and an estimate of the period during which care will be provided, including a schedule if leave is to be taken intermittently or if it will be necessary for you to work less than a full schedule:

_____ _____
(Employee Signature) (Date)

A **"Serious Health Condition"** means an illness, injury impairment, or physical or mental condition that involves one of the following:

1. Hospital Care

    Inpatient care (i.e., an overnight stay) in a hospital, hospice, or residential medical care facility, including any period of incapacity[2] or subsequent treatment in connection with or consequent to such inpatient care.

2. Absence Plus Treatment

    (a) A period of incapacity[2] of **more than three consecutive calendar days** (including any subsequent treatment or period of incapacity[2] relating to the same condition), that also involves:

    (1) **Treatment[3] two or more times** by a health care provider, by a nurse or physician's assistant under direct supervision of a health care provider, or by a provider of health care services (e.g., physical therapist) under orders of, or on referral by, a health care provider; or

    (2) **Treatment** by a health care provider on **at least one occasion** which results in a regimen of continuing **treatment[4]** under the supervision of the health care provider.

3. Pregnancy

    Any period of incapacity due to pregnancy, or for prenatal care.

Appendix C

4. Chronic Conditions Requiring Treatments

   A chronic condition which:

   (1) Requires **periodic visits** for treatment by a health care provider, or by a nurse or physician's assistant under direct supervision of a health care provider;

   (2) Continues over an **extended period of time** (including recurring episodes of a single underlying condition); and

   (3) May cause **episodic** rather than a continuing period of incapacity[2] (e.g., asthma, diabetes, epilepsy, etc.).

5. Permanent/Long-term Conditions Requiring Supervision

   A period of incapacity[2] which is **permanent or long-term** due to a condition for which treatment may not be effective. The employee or family member must be **under the continuing supervision of, but need not be receiving active treatment by, a health care provider**. Examples include Alzheimer's, a severe stroke, or the terminal stages of a disease.

6. Multiple Treatments (Nonchronic Conditions)

   Any period of absence to receive **multiple treatments** (including any period of recovery therefrom) by a health care provider or by a provider of health care services under orders of, or on referral by, a health care provider, either for **restorative surgery** after an accident or other injury, **or** for a condition that **would likely result in a period of incapacity**[2] **of more than three consecutive calendar days in the absence of medical intervention or treatment**, such as cancer (chemotherapy, radiation, etc.), severe arthritis (physical therapy), kidney disease (dialysis).

---

[3] Treatment includes examinations to determine if a serious health condition exists and evaluations of the condition. Treatment does not include routine physical examinations, eye examinations, or dental examinations.

[4] A regimen of continuing treatment includes, for example, a course of prescription medication (e.g., an antibiotic) or therapy requiring special equipment to resolve or alleviate the health condition. A regimen of treatment does not include the taking of over-the-counter medications such as aspirin, antihistamines, or salves; or bed-rest, drinking fluids, exercise, and other similar activities that can be initiated without a visit to a health care provider.

APPENDIX D

TYPES OF LEAVE

Short-Term Disability Benefits

Policy

[Employer]'s short-term disability plan is a benefit that provides partial pay (one-half of weekly wages up to a maximum benefit as determined by state law) for employees who are unable to work due to non-work related illness, injury, or disability, after an absence of more than 7 consecutive calendar days. Benefits begin on the 8th day of disability and continue for related absences up to a maximum of 26 weeks. If the employee returns to work and the disability recurs within 90 days, the employee does not have to wait the 7 days; disability benefits will begin immediately.

Guidelines

- A disability claim form, which can be obtained from **[Insert name of employer contact]**, must be filed with **[Insert name of employer contact]** within 20 days after becoming disabled. A short-term disability leave must be certified by a physician's or licensed health care professional's statement identifying the nature of the disability, and stating or estimating the date when the employee will be able to return to work. If the employee cannot return on that date, another statement from a physician or licensed health care professional, with a new return date, will be required. Employees will not be able to return to work without submitting to **[Insert name of employer contact]** a note from a physician or licensed health professional authorizing the employee's return.

- **[Employer]** reserves the right to confirm the necessity for disability leave by requiring the employee to receive a second or third opinion by a doctor of the Company's choice. **[Employer]** will assume any costs for additional examinations that are not paid by the insurance carrier.

- **[Employer]** will make an attempt to return an employee who is returning from a short-term disability leave to the same or similar job, at the same salary that the employee held prior to the leave. Under some circumstances, however, permanent replacement during a leave may be required, or in some instances, staffing requirements may change. Therefore, unless an employee is entitled to return to the same or an equivalent position under the Family and Medical Leave Act, a job cannot be guaranteed when the employee is ready to return to work from a short-term disability leave. In the event the employee is not entitled to return to the same or an equivalent position under the Family and Medical Leave Act and a position is not available or if the employee chooses not to return to work, upon the expiration of the disability leave, the employee will be terminated. If an employee does not return from a short-term disability leave, the termination date is the last day that the employee was authorized to return or the date the employee notifies his/her supervisor he/she is not returning, whichever is sooner. Such employees may be considered for reemployment. An employee who returns to work following a short-term disability leave will be considered as having continuous service.

Military Leave

Policy

An employee who is a member of the United States Army, Navy, Air Force, Marines, Coast Guard, a member of the National Guard, a member of the Reserves or Public Health Service will, where a specified period of active or reserve duty is mandatory, be granted a leave of absence in accordance with the applicable military leave law.

Procedure

- Upon receipt of orders for active or reserve duty, the employee should notify his/her supervisor, as well as **[Insert name of employer contact]**,

Appendix D 103

immediately and he/she must submit a copy of his/her orders to his/her supervisor and the _____ Department.

Employer Option

> Does Employer want to pay its employees for any time spent on military leave, e.g., the difference between the employee's regular salary and military pay for up to two weeks?

Jury & Witness Duty

Policy

A leave of absence for jury duty will be granted to any employee who has been notified to serve. An employee on jury duty is expected to report to work any day he/she is excused from jury duty. All employees summoned to court as a witness will be given the necessary time off, but without pay. Employees will be permitted to utilize accrued vacation time for this purpose.

Procedure

- The employee should immediately notify his/her supervisor, as well as the _____ Department on the day following the employee's receipt of a summons to serve on a jury or a subpoena to appear as a witness. Additionally, a copy of the notice to serve should be attached to the employee's attendance record for attendance purposes.

- Upon the employee's return from jury or witness duty, the employee must notify **[Insert name of employer contact]**. Employees absent for jury duty must submit a signed Certificate of Jury Service indicating the number of days served.

- Employees who are excused from jury or witness duty service early on any particular day must contact **[Insert name of employer contact]** to determine if they should report to work.

Note

If the Jury Duty falls at a time when the employee cannot be away from work, the court may allow the employee to choose a more convenient time to serve if he/she makes a request in accordance with the court's procedures.

Employer Option

> Does Employer want to grant employees pay while on jury duty or witness duty beyond the state requirement?

Voting Leave

Policy

An employee will be granted time off to vote in accordance with all state election law requirements.

Procedure

- If an employee has four consecutive hours either between the opening of the polls in his or her community and the beginning of the regular workday, or between the end of the regularly scheduled workday and the closing of the polls, the employee has sufficient time outside his or her regular work shift with which to vote.

- If there is not sufficient time off outside a shift, an employee may request time off to vote in a direct primary, presidential or general election. An employee may take the necessary time to vote at the beginning or end of the shift, whichever requires the least amount of time off from work. Up to two hours of voting leave time per election will be paid. Voting leave is not considered time worked, and therefore, will not be used in the calculation of overtime.

- An employee requiring time off to vote is required to notify [Insert company contact] not more than 10 nor less than 2 working days before the day of the election.

Appendix D

Vacation Leave

Policy

Time away from work to relax and pursue special interests is important to everyone. All full-time employees are eligible for paid vacation. During the first calendar year of employment at **[Employer]**, full-time employees who start work prior to July 1st will be eligible for vacation in the same calendar year after completing three months of service, according to the following schedule:

Schedule for First Calendar Year of Employment:

Hire Date	Number of Working Days for each Month of Work	
January 1–March 31	$5/_{12}$ of a day	(For example, if the employee started in January, he/she would have accrued 5 days by December; if the employee started in April, he/she would have accrued 3 days by December.)
April 1–June 30	$3/_{12}$ of a day	
July 1–December 31	0	

Full-time employees will be eligible for vacation in the following calendar year, after completing three months of service, based upon the following schedule:

After the First Calendar Year of Employment:

Length of Service	Number of Working Days for each month of work	Total Vacation Days if worked throughout year
2nd through 4th calendar year	$5/_6$	10
5th through 14th calendar year	$1 1/_4$	15
15th through 25th calendar year	$1 2/_3$	20
26th and each subsequent calendar year	$2 1/_{12}$	25

Employer Option

Does Employer want to give part-time employees any vacation allowance? Does Employer want to provide for advance vacation pay?

Guidelines

- Employees should utilize all of their allotted vacation time during the calendar year because, except in special circumstances, employees will not be permitted to carry vacation time not used into the following year. In other words, vacation time not used is not preserved. Where special business necessity requires an exception, prior approval must be given by **[Insert name of employer contact]**.

Employer Option

Does Employer want to allow employees to carry over any unused vacation time into the following vacation year?

- Based upon department needs, every effort will be made to grant an employee the vacation dates he/she requests.
- When a Company holiday falls during a scheduled vacation, it is not counted as a vacation day.

Guidelines for Vacation Pay upon Termination

Policy

Employees leaving _____ due to voluntary resignation, retirement or dismissal may be eligible to receive payment for vacation that has been accrued but not used. [Generally, in order for a resigning employee to qualify for payment of unused vacation, the employee must give at least two weeks notice and must work throughout the notice period; otherwise, the vacation pay will be forfeited.]

Unused vacation pay is calculated according to this formula:

Earned Vacation − Vacation Taken = Unused Vacation

Definition of Earned Vacation:

$$\frac{\text{Yearly Vacation Allowance}}{12 \text{ Months}} \times \text{Months of Service Completed that Calendar Year} = \text{Earned Vacation}$$

Appendix D

Employer Option

> Does Employer want to allot payment of unused vacation time where employee does not give notice prior to resigning?

Absence Due to Illness

Policy

To keep the business and each department running smoothly and efficiently, it is important that every employee be on the job on time regularly. For this reason, careful attention is given to promptness, absence record and overall dependability.

[Employer] recognizes, however, that an employee may occasionally be disabled by injury or illness. As a result, the Absence Due to Illness and Disability Policies are designed to provide protection to employees against loss of income during unavoidable illness or injury.

All full-time employees who are unable to perform their jobs due to illness or injury are eligible for salary continuance (reduced by any amount received from State Disability Benefits) according to the following schedule:

Length of Service   Salary Continuance

Employer Option

> Does Employer want to provide for salary continuance beyond state disability insurance? What does Employer want to provide?

Guidelines

- Employees unable to report to work due to illness must telephone their supervisor directly, each day of their absence, no later than one half hour after their scheduled arrival time. If their supervisor is not available, the _____ Department should be contacted. If an employee is unable to make the call personally, a family member or a friend should contact the supervisor. An employee who fails to contact his/her immediate supervisor or [Insert name of employer contact] may be considered as having voluntarily resigned. This policy must be followed unless an exception has been made for a particular absence, and a written memo to this effect has been sent to the _____ Department.

- Once an employee is out sick for 5 consecutive work days he/she must also notify **[Insert name of employer contact]** so that a short-term disability benefits claim form can be sent to him/her. Failure to do so may jeopardize salary continuance under the Absence Due to Illness or disability benefits.

- If **[Employer]** has questions about the nature or length of an employee's disability, a written confirmation from a physician or licensed health care professional may be required.

Bereavement Leave

Policy

In the unfortunate event of a death in the immediate family, a leave of absence of up to ___ days with pay will be granted.

For this purpose, immediate family is defined as:
Spouse
Child
Step-child
Parents (including in-laws), step-parents
Siblings, step-siblings
Grandparents
Grandchildren

Employer Option

Does the employer want to include significant others and same-sex partners?

Procedure

- Employees should make their supervisor aware of their situation. In turn, the supervisor should notify **[Insert name of employer contact]** of the reason and length of the employee's absence.

- Upon returning to work, the employee must record his/her absence as a Bereavement Leave on his/her attendance record.

Appendix D

Personal Leave (Paid)

Policy

All full-time employees who have been employed at **[Employer]** for more than one calendar year are eligible for ___ paid personal days per year, to be used for doctor's visits, religious observance, moving, etc. During the first calendar year of employment at **[Employer]**, personal days are calculated based on the following schedule:

Schedule for First Year of Service:

Hire Date		
	January 1 — June 30	___ day(s)
	July 1 — December 31	___ day(s)

Guidelines

- Personal days generally are not approved before an employee has been employed at **[Employer]** for at least three months. They are to be used at the employee's convenience with his/her supervisor/manager's advance approval.
- Under no circumstances will payment in lieu of time off be given and no pay is provided for personal days not taken when an employee terminates.

Employer Option

Does the employer want to give part-time employees any personal time?

Personal Leave (Unpaid)

Policy

Should a situation arise that temporarily prevents an employee from working, he/she may be eligible for a personal Leave of Absence without pay. However, employees must be employed for at least three months prior to the requested leave.

Any request for a leave of absence without pay must be submitted in writing and it is reviewed on a case-by-case basis by your supervisor/manager and the _____ Department. The decision to approve or disapprove is based on the circumstances, the length of time requested, the employee's job performance and attendance and punctuality record, the reasons for the leave, the effect the employee's absence will have on the work in the department and the expectation that the employee will return to work when the leave expires.

Leaves of absence will be considered only after all vacation and personal time have been exhausted. The duration of a leave of absence, if granted, is according to the following schedule:

Length of Service	Allowable Leave of Absence (number of months without pay_
Under ____ years	Up to ____ months
____ years and over	____ month for every year of service

Continuing Benefit Plan Coverage

While on a personal unpaid leave of absence, employee's medical coverage will end on the 1st day of the month following the start of such leave. Employees will have the opportunity of continuing their benefits for a maximum period of 18 months by paying the monthly premiums as required by COBRA legislation (see COBRA policy). [Credit for the profit sharing plan will not be given for the time spent on leave.]

Unemployment Insurance benefits cannot be collected while on a leave of absence without pay.

Salary Action

Any planned salary increase for an employee returning from a leave of absence without pay will be deferred by the length of the leave.

Vacation and Personal Time

During the calendar year that an employee takes a leave of absence without pay, vacation credit is not accrued while on leave. Accrued vacation and personal days must be used before a leave of absence without pay will be granted.

Performance Appraisal

The normal performance appraisal date of an employee on a leave of absence without pay will be extended by the length of the leave.

Appendix D

Returning/Not Returning from a Leave

Due to the nature of our business **[Employer]** cannot guarantee either that an employee's job will remain available or that a comparable position will exist when return from leave is sought. When an employee is ready to return from a leave of absence without pay, every effort will be made to reinstate the employee to his/her former position or to one with similar responsibilities.

Option 1: [If the position or a similar position is not available, the Company will search for a suitable position for 30 days from the date the leave was to officially end. The employee will not be paid for this time. If the employee has not been placed by the end of this period, he/she will be terminated.]

or

Option 2: [If the position or a similar position is not available, the employee will be terminated.]

An employee who returns to work following a leave will be considered as having continuous service. If an employee does not return from a leave of absence without pay, the termination date is the last day of the authorized leave period or the date the employee notifies his/her supervisor/manager he/she is not returning, whichever is sooner. Such employees may be considered for reemployment.

Holidays

All full-time employees (including those in initial employment period) are eligible for ___ paid holidays per year as follows:

New Year's Day	January
Martin Luther King Day	January
President's Day	February
Memorial Day	May
Independence Day	July
Labor Day	September
Columbus Day	October
Veteran's Day	November
Thanksgiving	November
Christmas	December

At the end of each year the holiday schedule for the coming year will be posted on the Bulletin Board.

Where a holiday falls on a weekend, it will be observed on either the preceding Friday or following Monday.